LC
4069.6　Newton, Eunice Shaed.
.N48　　　The Case for improved
1982　　　college teaching.

DISCARD

THE CASE FOR IMPROVED
COLLEGE TEACHING

THE CASE FOR IMPROVED COLLEGE TEACHING:

Instructing High-Risk College Students

by
Eunice Shaed Newton

VANTAGE PRESS
New York / Washington / Atlanta
Los Angeles / Chicago

FIRST EDITION

All rights reserved, including the right of
reproduction in whole or in part in any form.

Copyright © 1982 by Eunice Shaed Newton

Published by Vantage Press, Inc.
516 West 34th Street, New York, New York 10001

Manufactured in the United States of America
ISBN: 533-04812-5

Library of Congress Catalog Card No.: 80-52985

To Isham Gregory Newton

CONTENTS

Preface ix
Introduction xiii

1. Perspectives on Instructional Systems Design 1
2. Perceptions of High-Risk College Students 10
3. Instructional Systems in American Higher Education: Private-Traditional, Land-Grant-State, Black, Community 18
4. An Instructional Paradigm for High-Risk College Students 34
5. Taking Stock—Meeting the Challenge 69

Appendixes
   A. Syllabus in Basic English/Threshold Level 85
   B. The Literate Demands of a Typical College Textbook 92
   C. Levels and Dimensions of Reading Comprehension Applicable to All Types of Discourse 95
   D. The Directed Reading Activity (DRA) Adapted to College Studies 98

References 103

PREFACE

Interpreters of trends and policies in American higher education have traced what they perceive to be a chain reaction from the civil rights movement in the 1950s to the student revolution and accompanying campus unrest in the 1960s. The latter, in turn, is believed to have contributed to the extension of equal educational opportunity and accessibility in the 1970s to groups in our society that were formerly not viewed as "college material."

It is a well documented and publicized fact that large numbers of these newcomers to American higher education do not possess the academic prerequisites for success in learning tasks in conventional college settings. And many of these nontraditional entrants who are first-generation college matriculators have difficulty in adjusting because they lack realistic personal perspectives on the goals of traditional higher education.

What has been publicized with considerably less candor and thoroughness, however, is the fact that few institutions of higher education were and are prepared to conduct productive learning programs for their underprepared enrollees. Thus, it is not an overstatement to say that high-risk students' unreadiness for postsecondary studies is possibly exceeded in American higher education by equally manifest faculty unreadiness. This is why K. Patricia Cross has called for a "revolution in college teaching."

Some colleges and universities, nonetheless, have experienced greater success than others in accommodating and adapting to the needs of increased numbers of high-risk students. Black and urban community colleges, which have enrolled for many years predominantly minority and disadvantaged students, historically have coped with student diversity with varying degrees of success. These more or less nontraditional higher education institutions espouse approaches to teaching and learning that differ markedly from conventional elitist college education. And in this monograph I shall identify their philosophical orientations and utilize some of their prototype instructional strategies.

In spite of the fact that precollege underpreparation continues to burgeon throughout our country, colleges have been dilatory in developing appropriate instructional systems for their high-risk students. And even today, few issues in higher education can generate as much emotional debate as the quality of undergraduate teaching. At this point in time, therefore, there are few models of effective teaching-learning practices for new college entrants who need transitional development. Fortunately, however, for the purposes of this monograph, some notable exceptions to traditional college teaching emerged in the 1970s, largely under the sponsorship of the federal Fund for the Improvement of Postsecondary Education (FIPSE). Guides from FIPSE experiences and publications naturally will be included in the final synthesis of this monograph's paradigm.

For the most part, when institutions of higher education initially attempt to accommodate underprepared entrants, "remedial-compensatory" instructional systems are conceptualized and used. The limitations of these systems to date in ameliorating the issues and problems of high-risk students should be noted at this point (although an extended discussion of this matter will be presented in chapter three). Despite the circumscribed results secured from remedial-compensatory programs (primarily in skills-mastery programs for students with specific deficits in the tools-of-learning), properly utilized and subsumed under a broader instructional paradigm, remedial-compensatory skills-mastery programs have a substantive contribution to make to the development of high-risk students.

The primary purpose of this monograph is to formulate a critically needed model for college instruction which proposes both theoretical and pragmatic programs through which to address adequately the learning exigencies of today's high-risk college population. Inherent in this paradigm is the implication that many of the instructional strategies for high-risk students are broadly applicable to teaching and learning in undergraduate classrooms for conventional college students. In essence, the rationale and strategies herein presented for teaching today's underprepared students basically constitute as well a case for revising outmoded instructional practices for all students in American higher education.

In this proposed instructional model, I assess, adopt, adapt, and synthesize salient elements from remedial-compensatory models, traditional didactic procedures, and innovative college teaching procedures into a multidimensional instructional system. This methodological mosaic, which I choose to call *developmental-personalized instruction*, is undergirded with formative and normative research concerning human growth and development, learning theory, and cognitive styles. This instructional system recognizes the adult status of college students, and thus stresses the proven guides from andragogical principles. And lastly, all elements in this proposed paradigm manifest an awareness of the college student's needs for a constellation of cognitive and effective skills that provide coping behaviors and marketable abilities equal to the demands of this age of accelerating change.

In the development of this monograph, I have relied upon and synthesized more than forty years of teaching-learning experiences in a multiplicity of educational settings, ranging from the primary grades in public schools to postdoctoral teaching in different regions of the United States and abroad. Especially valuable have been some twenty-two years of administrative and instructional services for high-risk college students in skills-mastery and conventional studies in developing institutions. This monograph, therefore, reflects my varied practical experience germane to the subject, blended with citations and interpretations of significant, related literature.

Since corollary objectives in this monograph are to generate increased understanding of the profiles of high-risk students, and to espouse a change in conventional ways of thinking about the role and mission of higher education, I decided to use the essay rather than documented exposition as the vehicle of rhetorical presentation. The experiential and impressionistic views which are expressed along with research resources, however, are adequately buttressed by an extensive bibliography.

In addition to faculties who work directly with high-risk students in specialized programs, this monograph may be of some value to members-at-large in the college community who wish a contemporary view of optimal teaching-learning models. Whether in developing institutions or in the more elite bastions of liberal education, there is probably some aspect of this call for "a revolution in college teaching" that may serve the college instructor who desires it.

I gratefully acknowledge my indebtedness to the faculty and staff of the Center for Academic Reinforcement at Howard University for the major role which they played in the maturation and refinement of my perspectives on developmental-personalized instruction for high-risk college students.

I acknowledge, also, a special debt to the Robert R. Moton Memorial Institute, Inc., and the Moton Center for Independent Studies. As a recipient of a Moton Fellowship for 1979-1980, in an atmosphere of enlightened concern, I was able to think through, clarify, and develop my convictions about needed changes in undergraduate teaching.

Washington, D.C.
May 1980

INTRODUCTION

Social psychologists have noted for many years that when individuals who have anomalous characteristics gain membership in a long-established institution in a structured society, reactions to the deviant newcomers follow highly predictable patterns. Some veteran members reject the new entrants immediately with hostility; on the other hand, a few receive them with missionary zeal. Some regular members studiously avoid acknowledging the very existence of the new-type members, and only a minority of the established members begin seriously to address the attendant issues and problems.

Beginning in the late 1960s, when large numbers of students previously not considered to be "college material" began to gain access to American higher education, many of these so-called high-risk students were viewed as anomalies in traditional higher education communities. These nontraditional newcomers come largely from low socioeconomic strata and/or ethnic minorities, included more women, and were somewhat older than their former counterparts. Many college administrators and faculties continue to react to their presence with varying degrees of trepidation, hostility, and frustration, and for large numbers of these high-risk students the "open door" has become a "revolving door."

When the Congress of the United States passed the Morrill Acts in 1862 and 1890, the mission of higher education in America was extended to serve a need in the society-at-large for the application of scientific research to industrial and agricultural development. Thus, the service functions of higher education emerged, and the agricultural and mechanical arts became legitimate college studies in the latter part of the nineteenth century. Similarly, there is no reason not to believe that American higher education cannot again respond to the present critical need for another extension of its present purposes. Meeting the learning requirements of today's nontraditional college students will necessitate not only revisions in instructional strategies, but also a redefinition of the mission of traditional colleges and universities.

When Alvin Toffler confronted the reading public in 1970 with a perception of the technological status of our way of life in the waning decades of the twentieth century, it catapulted us, ready or not, into recognizing that "the future is now." We were brought to see that unprecedented scientific changes within a very brief period of time had disoriented many of the basic institutions in the industrial world. The field of education received a full measure of "future shock," and it has been slow to effect the changes that will provide the kind of education for students in a fluid society. And higher educational institutions in America have been markedly slower than the lower educational levels to recognize the student's need for a different type of intellectual development for coping with accelerated change.

K. Patricia Cross in the 1970s directed American higher education to a heightened level of perception and challenge concerning new-type college students. She insists that we must go beyond education for *all* to education for *each*. A response in some measure to Cross's call for an "instructional revolution" to meet the demands for productive learning by high-risk students is one of the principal motives for writing this monograph.

Chapter one, "Perspectives on Instructional Systems Design," presents theoretical and experiential views on the *why, what, who, how,* and *how well* of instructional systems. The chapter begins with analysis of the nature and role of models in any structured institution, and lays the foundation for the discussion of the development of paradigms in educational programs. Following the discussion of paradigms are brief reviews of the essential components in an instructional system: The *why*—purpose, raison d'etre, and goals; The *what*—content and objectives; The *who*—profile of clients; The *how*—the delivery-system (organization, methods, techniques); The *how well*—assessment and evaluation processes.

"Perceptions of High-risk College Students," chapter two, describes the personal and demographic identities of high-risk college students. The difficulties attendant to selecting a title by which to refer to this new student population are discussed, and my preferred labels are presented and justified. Out of the welter of literature about why high-risk students are underprepared for higher education, I synthesized some noteworthy views into a few thesis statements.

Chapter three, "Instructional Systems in Higher Education: Pri-

vate-Traditional, Land-Grant-State, Black, Community," presents an overview of the salient characteristics of instructional procedures in each of those higher educational institutions. The rationales and basic assumptions upon which each system is based is followed by an analysis of the strengths and weaknesses of each delivery system. And last, the features of each instructional system are identified which may be adoptable or adaptable to a paradigm for high-risk college students.

Chapter four presents my design for "an instructional paragidm for high-risk college students." The rationale and basic assumptions upon which the design rests and their synergetic relationships to the content, objectives, and instructional strategies are explained. The *sine qua non* features of an effective instructional system are discussed, and the ongoing evaluation processes are reviewed.

The final chapter, "Taking Stock—Meeting the Challenge," presents a plea for positive steps to be taken in all types of institutions of higher education to grapple systematically with the complex problems associated with upgrading undergraduate teaching. Lessons learned from the student, campus activism in American higher education in the 1960s as well as the various attempts at reconstructing academic policies in the 1970s are projected into curriculum practices for the 1980s and 1990s. The principal recommendation in the final report of the Carnegie Council on Policy Studies in Higher Education is strongly endorsed—the need for a systematic redefining of the goals and missions of American higher education to render more productive education by the year 2000. The chapter concludes with a vision of a kind of pluralistic instructional system needed in American higher education in order to help develop citizens able to cope in (Alvin Toffler's perception of) the imminent "third wave" civilization.

Appendix A is a prototype, basic English course syllabus. This skills-mastery package is illustrative of the principal instructional principles presented in chapter four.

Appendix B is a brief article, "The Literate Demands of a Typical College Textbook." It is included in the interest of sensitizing college teachers to the multiplicity of reading/thinking skills which the student must possess in order to read effectively standard, college texts.

Appendix C contains a condensed review entitled "Levels and Dimensions of Reading Comprehension Applicable to All Types of Discourse." Inasmuch as many college courses are in essence "reading courses," college teachers who understand the types and levels of the verbal/decoding skills should be able to guide learning with increased efficiency.

Appendix D presents another brief article on a topic important to the college teacher's repertory of instructional practices in serving students of vast academic diversity—"The Directed Reading Activity (DRA) Adapted to College Studies." The DRA is a widely recognized, innovative instructional aid of value to teachers in all college disciplines in guiding student comprehension of complex, highly structured, fact-saturated textbooks.

THE CASE FOR IMPROVED COLLEGE TEACHING

Chapter 1

PERSPECTIVES ON INSTRUCTIONAL SYSTEMS DESIGN

Introduction

In spite of the fact that the term *instructional systems design* has entered the realm of educational nomenclature only within the past decade, explicitly devised models and methods of instruction have been developed and used for centuries by philosophers and pedagogues. We may, for example, infer that Euclid had clearly established teaching procedures for guiding the sons of the pharaohs in the mastery of mathematics. Why else would he have reprimanded one of the reluctant learners with that most famous of educational put-downs: "There is no royal road to geometry"? And Aristotle's renowned method of deductive logic, which became the basis of scientific research and study in the Western world, is just another one among many classical examples of the antiquity of purposeful instructional strategies.

In more recent times, Johann Friedrich Herbart, Maria Montesorri, Jean Piaget, John Dewey, and Jerome Bruner all have developed and advocated models of learning and instruction. Each system in its own way contains a plan of operation to facilitate the acquisition by the student of habits and skills, information and knowledge, and attitudes and appreciations. An analysis of these philosophies and theories of instruction reveals that each includes in some measure provisions for (a) the transmission of information to the learner, (b) the reinforcement and storage of information within the learner, (c) the coding of information for retrieval, and (d) other elements that guide the learner to attain the desired objectives and/or goals.

In the United States since the latter decades of the nineteenth century, elementary school educators (and to a lesser extent those in the secondary schools) have recognized and encouraged the use of various instructional systems. On the other hand, higher educational circles in America have been almost completely indifferent to the role and importance of instructional practices in the attainment of the baccalaureate degree. In fact, if equal educational opportunity had not been extended in the 1960s to a more diverse student population than in prior years, even today there probably would be little evidence of a change in *traditional collegiate pedagogy*—principally authoritarian, didactic lectures.

Slowly but surely a broader concept of effective instruction is beginning to assume a level of importance commensurate with the present need for it. This elevation in the importance of college teaching is due largely to increased academic heterogeneity of the students, coupled with sharp criticisms of the quality of college teaching voiced by parents, state legislators, and students as the high cost of a college education continues to burgeon.

It is unlikely that the interest in effective instruction in higher education would have expanded in the 1970s as dramatically as it did without the support from various private, state, and federal funding agencies. At the national level, a 1972 report by the National Advisory Council on Education Professions Development focused pointedly upon the critical need for upgrading the training and performance of community college teachers. At the state level, funds have been earmarked increasingly by legislators for instructional improvement in higher education in the interest of making colleges more accountable.

In addition to money allocated by states and the federal government through such agencies as the Fund for the Improvement of Postsecondary Education (FIPSE) and the National Institute of Education (NIE), a number of private foundations have begun to allocate funds to individual colleges or through consortia for the single purpose of emphasizing faculty development in teaching. "The AAUP Project to Improve College Teaching" and "The Center for Research and Learning and Teaching" are notable examples of this trend.

Prominent in the American ideology is pride in our ability to develop new technologies or modify old practices to accommodate the demands and needs of our society. In the late 19th Century higher education responded positively to the demands of the Industrial Revolution for applied scientific know-how. In this era of unprecedented change why cannot American higher education again generate appropriate developments to meet the challenge of educating diverse student populations?

As the principles and steps unfold later regarding the planning process necessary to develop and deliver an instructional system for today's college students, it is anticipated that the sum-total will contribute in some measure to meeting the challenge.

The Nature and Role of Paradigms

Institutions in structured societies have certain distinguishable characteristics which are in essence an amalgam of their rules, policies, regulations, traditions, and general *modus operandi*. These factors and others in conjunction with their organized body of information, skills, and knowledge give each institution a distinct identity. Some of an organization's features are explicitly stated in written documents; other aspects of their identity can be inferred only from their interests, commitments, and activities. (See Kuhn, 1970, *passim*.)

Subsystems in institutions (as well as secondary and tertiary subsystems) may have clearly identifiable characteristics in addition to possessing the general identity of the parent organization. For example, a department of pediatrics in a hospital has its own specialized identity, policies, and functions while at the same time sharing the general identity of the entire hospital. And extending this illustration one step further, think of the unique roles and services of surgeons and nurses in pediatrics, which involves several strata of identities.

As an institution (or subsystem) performs its distinctive services in a society over a period of time, an image of it develops in the minds of the community. This image gradually solidifies and crystallizes, and then the society expects the institution to function in specifically defined ways. The institution's overall activities at this point become a "model," a "pattern," a "paradigm" of societal expectations of its role. And the model or paradigm of an institution not only undergirds the performance of its prescribed institutional role, but also the model contributes to the stability and effectiveness of the total society.

It is possible to apply quite broadly much of the foregoing discussion to the field of education in general, and specifically to a consideration of the nature and role of instructional paradigms. Educational institutions have clearly identifiable images. Societal expectations in the United States for each of the major levels—elementary and secondary schools, as well as for higher education—are easily distinguishable, are solidly entrenched, and are virtually unchanging. For the most part, the educational establishment in the United States on all levels is a conservative institution. Resistance to reform of its basic roles and functions has been long noted, but the increasing demands from the public that education become more resonant with the society as it really is may generate the necessary leverage for long-needed revisions.

Instructional System: Definition, Brief History, Structure

At the outset of this section, the term *instructional system* should be defined before the procedures for developing it are set forth. Inasmuch as no definition, regardless of its accuracy, can aptly describe anything completely, nonetheless by combining a standard dictionary definition of *system* with a pedagogical definition of *instruction,* a reasonably adequate meaning is derived: *an instructional system is a synergetic arrangement and combination of the purposes, goals, objectives, content, methods, techniques, materials-of-instruction, and evaluative processes to form a unified or organic whole to guide the learner toward attaining the objectives of the learning activities*.

The writer believes that the key word is *synergetic* in the foregoing definition, and that it sets an instructional system apart from traditional methodologies. Synergetic principles inherent in an instructional system provide for cohesive interrelatedness between all of the distinguishable elements and components. Elaborating on this synergetic principle, we find, therefore, that the purposes and goals are the foundation of the objectives and content; the objectives and content are the bases of the methods and techniques; the materials-of-instruction are appropriately supportive of the methods in which they are used; and the assessment and evaluative processes are inextricably related to all of the aforementioned entities.

A reference was made in the first section of this chapter to the venerable history of structured pedagogical methods. At this point there is perhaps some merit in presenting a brief historical review of the principal phases in the development of instructional systems. Gagne (1974), Briggs (1979), and others identify three major phases in the history of instructional systems. The centuries-long dominance of rote learning involving the lowest level of association of ideas and the lecture-method should be noted.

The first phase of the development of instructional systems may be termed "the period of individual scholars and authoritarian didacticism." This period stretched virtually unmodified from the Golden Age of Greece through the Medieval and Renaissance epochs all the way to the latter part of the nineteenth century. Its outstanding characteristic was the individual development by a classical scholar of his learned observations and studies which were logically organized into a treatise. The treatise was customarily delivered in verbatim lectures to the students, and with the coming of the Gutenberg era, the treatise became a textbook. The durability and ubiquity of this classical instructional mode in higher education stimulates fascinating conjectures, and it may be observed today ostensibly unchanged in many universities.

Beginning in the last two decades of the nineteenth century and continuing throughout the twentieth, the second developmental phase of instructional systems emerged. It may be termed "the period of collaborative scholarship and mass production of texts." Teams of scholars, either in the same or related fields of study, combined and integrated their research and writing into highly organized textbooks for commercial publication. As time passed, the textbooks increasingly contained so-called "instructional features"—chapter summaries, pre- and post-tests, glossaries, etc. In spite of the mass dissemination of structured information, which reinforced and augmented the professor and the extension of textbooks beyond the basic treatise, learning strategies remained in many colleges until quite recently essentially the same as they had been for centuries—the lecture, rote memorization and recitation—undifferentiated mass education.

The third and final phase in the historical development of structured teaching/learning procedures may be called "the period of systems-oriented instructional design." Dating roughly from the early 1960s when public education on all levels in the United States expanded massively and received unprecedented financial support, the systems approach to instructional development was initiated. At a later point in this monograph a comprehensive analysis will be presented of this newest mode of planning and delivering instructional services; however, at this juncture it is sufficient to summarize its significant features: (a) diagnosis and needs assessment are utilized unfailingly to establish what should be attained; (b) multiple learning strategies are supported by alternative media to meet the heterogeneous cognitive styles of the learners; (c) evaluation and assessment activities are related directly to the objectives of instruction; and (d) the system is adaptable and appropriate for individual faculty development, or for subsystem (departmental), or for a major institution (a college) to implement.

Steps in Designing an Instructional System

Designing an instructional system can be as involved or as simple as the intellectual stance of an educator, or a college, or a unit in a college wishes it to be. In the interest of simplifying a process that frequently becomes quite attenuated, the writer suggests that the desired results may be accomplished by negotiating five critical steps in response to five pivotal questions:

1. *Why* is the instructional system needed?
2. *What* is it attempting to accomplish?
3. *Who* is the population whose needs are to be met?
4. *How* shall the teaching/learning strategies be performed?
5. *How well* can the validity of the system be monitored and assessed?

The *why* question is customarily referred to in related literature as "the needs assessment" process, and it is generally considered to be the *sine qua non* upon which all elements and components of the system rest. In this regard, the purposes, goals, and mission of the college (or department, or course) will be identified, verified, and prioritized, and then related to the career goals of the students. The overriding thrust of the *Why* step is to answer the question: of what possible merit, value, worth, or contribution to student development is this instructional system?

The second step in designing an instructional system, the *what*, is in effect a translation of the *why*. As the instructor (or department, or college) attempts to project what is actually to be accomplished (attained, mastered, learned, internalized) by the students, he transforms the goals into measurable performance objectives. For example, a long-range goal may be to produce graduates who can cope adequately with the verbal proficiencies needed in their careers. A related immediate, short-range course-objective in a freshman composition course, on the other hand, may be to produce students who can develop a thesis (topic) sentence in at least three different types of paragraphs.

Chapter two in this monograph will present an extensive essay on the *who* in instructional systems design. At this point it is necessary only to say that the nature of the educational client pervades and controls every aspect of the teaching/learning program, and that it is critically important that instructors possess certifiable facts about the academic, intellectual, and personal characteristics of their students.

In two previous sections of this monograph, references have been made to the narrow, didactic, authoritarian lecture method that has been used for centuries as the standard instructional procedure in higher education. The *how* of college teaching has been in need of creative and substantive revision for years. The fourth step in designing an instructional system, the *how* is developed as a repertory of exemplary "instructional events or episodes" which experiential and research-based information have proved to be productive. Inasmuch as the central focus of chapter four will be to present an extensive analysis of the hallmarks of effective instruction for today's college students, at this point it is necessary only to review briefly some of the contemporary perceptions of optimum teaching-learning situations relevant to the *how* step.

Mary Anne Raywid (1977) has recently developed a unique, metaphoric portrayal of ideal learning situations. She contends that all teachers are governed consciously or unconsciously by a particular image or metaphor which contains his idea of the best way to guide learning. Raywid identifies five models that have gained wide acceptance in reform proposals and practices today. The bazaar model likens the ideal learning circumstance to visiting a marketplace and shopping for and amassing things in which one is interested. This model is at the heart of the British philosophy of "open education." John Holt's metaphor of the school as a "great smorgasbord of intellectual, artistic, creative, and athletic activities" is analogous to the foregoing model. (See Raywid, 1977.)

The second and third contemporary models which are antithetical to traditional sitting-and-listening education are the praxis and the siddhartha. In the former, there is an emphasis upon putting theory into practice, and students are thus involved in real work and vital community activities. Knowledge and action which are united whenever possible in field experiences bridge the gap between education and life, and the praxis model overcomes the isolation of school learning. The *Siddhartha* model could be termed the idiosyncratic or personal quest model as well. This instructional paradigm refers to the young man in Herman Hesse's novel whose inner compulsions lead him to seek fulfillment in a variety of self-directed ways. This model is virtually an extension of well-planned and executed personalized-individualized instructional strategies.

The fourth and fifth instructional models which Raywid reports are the amusement park and the "just-be." The amusement park model is similar to the bazaar concept, but it includes additionally a multiplicity of "barkers" who coerce, motivate, and direct the individual in a wide variety of things in which to actively participate. A high premium is placed on choice and on the alternatives to lock-step regimens. The *"just-be"* model, on the other hand, is essentially rooted in the counterculture movement of the 1960s, which stressed the value and importance of any and all types of experiences. At the heart of this model is the belief that one learns simply by and from existing—i.e., learning comes automatically from living. Advocates within recent years who have called for a "deschooling" of society strongly endorse the "just be" instructional paradigm. It is suggested by some "just be" advocates that John Dewey's memorable philosophical dictum, "education is life," is compatible with this model.

The five metaphoric instructional models presented in the foregoing summaries are just a few among many contemporary ways of perceiving and conducting teaching-learning situations. Each of the five is in some way a departure from the traditional college model of passive-student-active-teacher syndrome. And some elements of the philosophical assumptions which undergird these models will be embedded in the writer's design of an instructional paradigm in chapter four.

The final step in an instructional system, *how well*, historically has been the area which has received the least serious attention in American higher education on the undergraduate level. (The grade inflation scandals of the 1960s are a case in point.) Under the umbrella of the shibboleth and/or sacred cow, "academic freedom," traditional college professors have ignored most attempts to assess how well their courses lead to student attainment of the stated objectives. Fortunately, since the 1960s, educational accountability pressures from the general public are reaching the ivory towers, and the synergetic relationships between all aspects in an instructional system obtain in higher education today. The final section in chapter four addresses evaluation of instruction in college learning assistance programs and presents its issues, problems, and procedures.

Summary

This chapter has presented significant views, opinions, observations, conceptualizations, and judgments about the nature, role, and development of instructional systems. At first, the antiquity of structured methods of instruction was referred to, and the centuries-long persistence of traditional didacticism in higher education was noted.

The purposes and functions of models or paradigms in any societal institution were delineated, and the particular characteristics of instructional paradigms was presented. Then, an instructional system was defined, a brief historical review of the phases in the development of pedagogical methods was presented, and the unique features of "systems-oriented" instructional design were then provided.

Near the end, this chapter devoted a section to a discussion of the steps in designing an instructional system. It was suggested that the answers to five pivotal questions would elicit the necessary components of an instructional paradigm by individual faculty, a department, or an entire college team. Contemporary models of "ideal teaching-learning situations" that vary markedly from the traditional higher education genre were summarized briefly in the final section.

Chapter 2

PERCEPTIONS OF HIGH-RISK COLLEGE STUDENTS

Introduction

Literature about high-risk college students is both abundant and variegated, and an extensive review of it is beyond the purview of this monograph. Some pivotal information, nonetheless, about these newcomers to American postsecondary education will be summarized. Whether in the daily press or in the most abstruse professional journals, since the 1960s, educators as well as the general public have discussed, researched, and analyzed extensively the etiology and status of nontraditional newcomers to American higher education. Securing answers to two principal questions are the major foci of this literature: Who are the high-risk students, and what are their personal and demographic identities? And in this wealthiest nation in the world, in which astronomical quantities of tax dollars are spent for the support of education on all levels, how is it that thousands of students are academically underprepared for higher education?

Subjective speculations as well as hard empirical data on the identities of high-risk college students range over a full spectrum of views—from simplistic to complex, from benign to disaffected. Especially polarized are the writings about the reasons why the excellence of American precollege education has declined so precipitously and measurably within the past decade and a half. In this chapter an attempt is made to present a succinct yet balanced picture of the diverse positions about this target population. In addition to the writer's professional experience with and research on high-risk students, the works of K. Patricia Gross (1971) and Martha Maxwell (1979) serve as primary references in this synthesis.

Who Are the High-Risk Students?

Selecting a term by which to refer to nontraditional newcomers to higher education posed a problem for the writer, and the literature reports a similar problem faced by others on this subject. Finding a term which is appropriately descriptive and yet not demeaning is difficult. This is confirmed when the terms that are frequently used are examined: *minority, new-type, underprepared, open-admissions, miseducated, misprepared, undereducated, newcomers, academically disadvantaged, culturally disadvantaged, transitional, remedial,* and *high-risk*. Each term reflects an educational philosophy or a personal bias toward this student population which ranges from semiappropriate, to the euphemistic and derogatory. The terms *high-risk* and *underprepared* are used principally in this monograph because the writer found them to be defensible and the least deprecating. It may be argued that the term *high-risk* shifts the focus from the students and their deficiencies to the admissions criteria of the colleges and their assessments of the students' probability of success. The second preferred term, *underprepared*, has a high degree of validity, for many high-risk students today have demonstrable deficits in verbal and mathematical skills—the "tools-for-learning."

As preparation for noteworthy views in the literature about the personal and demographic identities of high-risk college students, another brief digression concerning labelings of these students may contribute to the overall understanding of this topic. The terms *high-risk* and *underprepared* are "relative," not "absolute." As Martha Maxwell has so aptly put it, one must never forget that what is high-risk at one institution may be low-risk at another; and what is underpreparation for one American college may be overpreparation for another. The 3,000 or so different two- and four-year American institutions of higher education have incredibly wide ranges in admissions criteria, academic emphases, and academic standards.

The relativity of the terms *high-risk* and *underprepared* increases substantially when differences in the academic rigor and prerequisites between courses in a college become interactive with the variables in students' pre-college preparation. Consider, momentarily, the following case: A student enrolls from a secondary school that had a strong program in English and a weak one in mathematics. The English language study program has prepared him for admission to the freshman composition course in college, and he progresses without incident in the first-year English sequences. On the other hand, since his secondary school required only two semesters of tenth grade mathematics (only one of which was algebra), he is drastically underprepared for the first, regular college mathematics course, "elementary functions"—a combination of college algebra and trigonometry. Since his prospective major field of study in the natural sciences requires proficiency in mathematics through calculus, it will take him at least two semesters of mathematical preparation in the college skills center to attain "readiness" for the initial mathematics course. This student is clearly low-risk and prepared at the time of matriculation for courses requiring verbal proficiency, but high-risk and underprepared in those requiring mathematical skills.

Clark Kerr (1963), more than fifteen years ago with exceptionally accurate prescience, identified today's high-risk students both as to number and character. It was his belief then that in this last quarter of the twentieth century the American university would have to undergo its second great transformation. (The first occurred during the last quarter of the nineteenth century when the land-grant college movement was conceptualized and initiated.) The second metamorphosis in American higher education, Kerr predicted, would have to be generated to accommodate unprecedented numbers of new-entrants who have a full range of personal and intellectual diversity. They are coming into postsecondary education primarily in response to the needs and demands of our rapidly changing technological, governmental, industrial, and social institutions for increased numbers of citizens who possess new dimensions of intellectual competencies.

It is difficult to comprehend the sheer magnitude of the recently increased enrollments in American higher education. By 1960, in the slightly more than three centuries since the founding of Harvard, the maximum annual enrollment in American colleges and universities had reached approximately three million students. By fall of 1979, in less than two decades, the enrollment in some 3,000 institutions of higher education exceeded 11 million by several hundred thousands. Should we be surprised, therefore, that this rapid growth in American higher education has proved to be a Herculean challenge? In fact, as K. Patricia Cross perceives it, what started as an approach to extending equality of access to college because of rising educational expectations and needs of our society has turned into an educational revolution involving all of higher education.

The verity of Cross's observation above strikes home quite pointedly when we review some of the personal and demographic data about the newcomers to higher education. And it must not be forgotten that almost half of the present 11 million enrollees in American institutions of higher education may be classified as high-risk or underprepared by some established criteria. The statements that follow summarize some of their most significant identifying qualities:

1. Almost two-thirds of the target population are first-generation college students; their parents have never attended college.

2. Blacks and other minorities constitute approximately 40 percent; the rest are Caucasians (a fact that is persistently disbelieved in both educational circles and the larger society).

3. The majority are from formerly underrepresented groups in American higher education—adults, women, lower socioeconomic levels, and ethnic-minorities.

4. The majority rank in the lowest one-third on admissions tests—CEEB, ETS, and ACT.

5. For the majority, the motivation for college arises from conservative interests—to get a better job, more money, and higher social status.

6. More than half of high-risk postsecondary students matriculate at two-year community colleges. (And approximately three-fourths of all black undergraduates enroll in community colleges or predominantly black institutions.)

7. Financial aid packages are vital to the economic survival of the majority of nontraditional students. Whether in private, land-grant, municipal, or community colleges, federal, state, and even municipal scholarships are needed if these students remain in college. (And with the current economic dislocations in America, higher educational institutions have found it important to their financial survival, also, to retain increased numbers of students as well as admit them.)

8. Although the data are not available on the precise number of high-risk students who actually graduate from higher educational institutions, the unverified information is that ten to twenty percent do "succeed" in college. (This concept of "success" means that they graduated from a four-year program within the expected eight semesters and perhaps one or two summers.) The plight of the eighty

to ninety percent who "fail" will be discussed in chapter three in connection with community colleges and remedial/compensatory models of college instruction.

Within less than two decades, the overall character of the student population in American higher education has changed extensively. In spite of the different terms by which the newcomers are identified, fully one-half of the current enrollment would not have measured up to pre-1960 standards of "good college material." Granted that American higher education has always enrolled limited numbers of students of diverse social, economic, and academic backgrounds, there is today in our colleges and universities virtually the full range of the normal curve of trait distribution. (It should be noted at this point that the predominantly black colleges in America have always had highly heterogeneous student populations. Since the 1960s, their students have increased primarily quantitatively. In chapter three some attention will be given, however, to problems of black colleges' recent problems of qualitative student differences.)

Who then are the high-risk college students? Today they are rapidly becoming what Horace Mann called "all of the children of all of the people." In nineteenth century America when the battle for free, tax-supported elementary education ensued, the elementary seven and eight grades became "the common school." From the 1870s to the 1930s, the American high school eventually became the common school, and twelve years of free, tax-supported education for all became a societal expectation. Within the past decade and a half, as the enrollment in America higher education has been more than triplicated by previously unimagined numbers and types of students, fourteen to sixteen years of free, tax-supported education have become the common school.

Reasons for Underpreparation for American Higher Education

In 1964 when college enrollments had begun to escalate by the admission of previously unsolicited students, Robert S. Morison (1964) referred to contemporary American higher education as "the knowledge industry." It may be inferred that his use of that metaphor foresaw the changing pattern of college matriculation as the decisive factor in altering higher educational institutions. Was Morison implying that the American university (had and/or must) shift consciously from its traditional preoccupation with the pursuit of knowledge and truth to at least a tacit acceptance of society's increasing expectation for it to serve as a "career factory" in meeting society's economic ends?

Whether or not one finds Morison's analogy to be neither appropriate nor palatable, the implication is virtually uncontestable—that as an industry, American higher education is substantially interested in "production." And being product- or production-oriented leads to an inherent interest in the "raw material" which is to be "processed." It is within this context, therefore, that we review the multiplicity of literature since the early 1960s that seeks to explain why American students are underprepared for higher educational studies.

The literature reports a wide variety of studies and analyses of the reasons for the escalating underpreparation for American higher education since the early 1960s. The studies range from simple to complex, from limited to comprehensive, and from empirical to speculative. An exhaustive review and analysis of this readily available literature is beyond the purview of this monograph; nonetheless, a summary of significant literature on precollege underpreparation follows.

Two definitive, landmark studies have been made of perceived reasons for the sharp increase within the past decade and a half in underpreparation for post-secondary education of American college-bound students. The statements that follow synthesize the central positions in regard to this topic as reported by K. Patricia Cross (1971) in her research for *Beyond the Open Door: New Students in Higher Education*, and the *Advisory Panel on the Scholastic Aptitude Score Decline* by the College Entrance Examination Board, which was chaired by Willard Wirtz (1977).

1. There are no simple, monolithic answers to questions about reasons for the post-1960 underpreparation of college-bound students in the United States. There is a veritable matrix of interrelated, inextricably involved personal, sociocultural, educational, and global factors that impact on this problem.

2. A virtual chain-reaction appears to operate between identified sociocultural factors associated with national and global dislocations of World War II that affect adversely the functions and standards of public elementary and secondary education. In turn, the deteriorating academic standards of the lower levels of public education appear to be related directly and indirectly to student performance on college entrance examinations.

3. The general decrease in traditional college preparatory courses

offered in American high schools since the 1960s is believed to be a significant factor in the fourteen-year downward spiral of SAT-M and SAT-V scores. In many instances, basic mathematical and verbal skills included in the SATs as well as the CEEB and ACT achievement examinations have been eliminated from current high school courses of study.

4. The civil rights movement and resulting federal legislation of the 1950s generated active college recruitment of students previously excluded because of low economic status. (Many of these students are black and from other minorities.) Federal and state financial aid packages of various types are today awarded on the basis of financial need, not academic merit as in the past. These grants have virtually eliminated former economic barriers to American higher education. The magnitude of this factor can be assessed when we consider the reports that financial aid increased 6,000 percent from 1954-1974, and that federal Basic Educational Opportunity Grants are proposed to increase to 75 percent (rather than half) of a student's educational costs by 1985 (*The Chronicle*, 9/4/79).

5. The exact nature of the role and influence of television in contemporary American society has not as yet been comprehensively defined. Educators and the general public as well, nonetheless, believe that television has profoundly influenced American values, outlook, preferences, desires, education, and perhaps even our views of reality. The Wirtz Report on reasons for the decline in SAT scores generally concurs with the belief that television may be an identifiable factor. Without concurring entirely with Marshall McLuhan (1965), it is probably fair to say that some tangentially related fallout from living in this "post-Gutenberg" era characterized by nonlineal communication has contributed in some way to a decline in the mastery of traditional academic studies. (Our educational system continues to be bound primarily to print media.)

Summary

Within the past two decades, as the egalitarian thrusts of the 1950s generated mammoth increases in higher educational enrollment in America, the characteristics of the students who were previously excluded have been documented exhaustively. Interpretations of the research on these newcomers to higher education varies widely, but the majority of it acknowledges that the findings on underpreparation for postsecondary education involve a full measure of sociological, psychological, and economic factors.

Some serious questions have not been addressed squarely by researchers in regard to the concern of this chapter, and they will be raised at this point because American higher education must eventually come to grips with them:

1. Is the concept of "underpreparedness" statistically valid in light of the distribution of traits (cognitive, affective, or motor) in any random population? (The myth of monodimensional academic prowess as being predictive of later success must be critically examined.)

2. Is it feasible and/or rational to continue trying to fit "twenty-first century newcomers" to "nineteenth century higher education"? Would it not make more sense to redefine and restructure American higher education in light of the current societal *Zeitgeist* and *Weltanschauung*?

Chapter 3

INSTRUCTIONAL SYSTEMS IN AMERICAN HIGHER EDUCATION: PRIVATE-TRADITIONAL, LAND-GRANT-STATE, BLACK, COMMUNITY

Introduction

Of the three principal missions of American higher education—research, service, and teaching—the last historically has not been customarily rewarded as a significant factor in professional recognition or faculty promotion and tenure. In fact, college teaching has been considered for the most part to be a natural by-product of the interaction between great scholars and their students, which should be left to the idiosyncratic whims and styles of the professor. Only within the past two decades, therefore, largely due to external pressures, has American higher education seriously considered the issues and problems concerning the quality of undergraduate teaching and learning. And only within the past ten years have there transpired on this matter creditable discussion, research, analysis, and action (see *Change—Reports on Teaching, No. 1, 2, 3, 4, 5,* March 1976, July 1976, January 1977, July 1977, January 1978).

The recent upsurge of interest in higher educational instructional practices may be traced directly to two events. First, steep unprecedented increases in the costs of postsecondary education have caused state legislatures as well as the general public to demand greater accountability in all institutions of higher education. In essence, the public is asking: What are the youth getting for their money? And second, the more than tripled student enrollments since 1960 have presented American higher education with clients possessing previously unimagined academic and attitudinal heterogeneity. Student populations of such obvious diversity require productive, creative teaching of hitherto unprovided dimensions.

There are wide differences in size, organization, facilities, faculty, mission, student characteristics, academic emphases, and history among the approximately 3,000 accredited degree-granting American institutions of higher education (two-year colleges, four-year colleges and universities). Additionally, they vary markedly in the instructional systems which are customarily utilized by their faculties in teaching-learning interactions. In this chapter, the instructional systems of four types of American higher educational institutions will be discussed: private-traditional, land-grant-State, black, and community; and their basic rationales, assumptions, and dominant positive and negative characteristics will be presented.

Private-Traditional College Instruction

Private-traditional, Ivy League-type institutions of higher education, founded in some instances in colonial days or during the early days of our republic, reflect even today the European influences on American postsecondary education. More than in any other type of American college or university, the private-traditional institution's academic programs rest upon two overriding assumptions: (1) that the entering student has mastered the "tools-of-learning"—verbal, mathematical, study/thinking; and (2) that the student has both the interest and dedication to devote himself consciously to the pursuit of increased knowledge in a discipline of his choice.

In a lucid essay on the contemporary American college of liberal arts, William C. Devane (1964) discusses convincingly how continental and English institutions for centuries were justifiably based on the two foregoing assumptions. For centuries they have had the *lycée*, the *Gymnasium*, or a Harrow or Eton upon which to undergird their academic programs. The exclusive European secondary schools have prepared a microcosmic élite for independent learning in the university through programs of studies which are comparable to the curriculum in few if any American undergraduate colleges. With students so ably prepared for advanced study and learning, the lecture method used in European universities is admirably appropriate for use as the primary vehicle through which to transmit information and knowledge.

With few exceptions, contemporary American private-traditional institutions of higher education use, also, the lecture method, with limited recitation and discussion as their principal instructional tool. This method is used in spite of the fact that American precollege preparation rarely compares favorably with European secondary education. And the large number of American college freshmen who fail or drop out after one or two semesters attests to how traditional instructional practices serve as indirect, postadmissions criteria for discriminating in American higher education.

Henry Seidel Canby (1936) vividly portrayed from first-hand experience the all too frequent aridity, indifference, and severity of traditional college lectures. He found equally nonproductive the triviality and perfunctoriness of student recitation. And what Canby reported in his day largely prevails today. McLeish (1968) and Keller (1974), among others, have concluded from research on lecturing and learning that for the majority of students, even under ideal conditions, the lecture method is not the most effective means of disseminating information. Before summarizing research concerning the positive and negative features of the lecture method, there may be some merit at this point in reviewing briefly the primary skills and competencies a student should have mastered in order to benefit maximally from this instructional strategy. Readiness for learning from the lecture method includes a repertory of the following "learning-to-learn" skills: (1) the ability to focus on the business-at-hand through consciously screening-out unrelated distractions; (2) skill in "active," "reconstructive" listening—i.e., alertly decoding the lecturer's expressed ideas through associating, relating, accepting, rejecting, analyzing, speculating, and connecting them to previously learned materials; (3) writing in note form (i.e., abbreviated clauses, phrases, key-words) the dominant ideas and most important facts; (4) translating and converting the information into synonymous and analogous terms for multiple-retrieval storage; and (5) systematically and periodically modifying, amending, reviewing, and synthesizing lecture notes for reinforcement, reorganization, and recategorization into the larger context as the course develops.

The student's mastery of the foregoing "learning-to-learn" skills is secured through planned, systematic, directed instruction and practice in both elementary and secondary school. The literature suggests, however, that even students who enter higher education with these requisite competencies will not attain unalloyed results from the lecture method; and for large numbers of high-risk students who enroll generally lacking these study skills, early failure is a precluded consequence.

The lecture method has some strengths as well as some weaknesses, which have been analyzed extensively in recent years as higher education has begun to focus upon improving the quality of undergraduate teaching. (See Trent, 1973; Lee, 1967; Milton, 1972.) The following are some recognized positive features and contributions of the lecture as a teaching/learning strategy:

1. Audible language embodies vicarious experiences and information with life through the vocal techniques of stress, cadence, rhythm, poise, and phrasing in a manner that is impossible for visible language in textbooks to do. A multitude of implicit meanings is conveyed by a lecturer who possesses a repertory of tonal pyrotechnics. The truly important ideas in a lecture can be emphasized and highlighted, therefore, and may serve as a means of comprehension and an aid to retention and recall for the student who has mature listening proficiency.

2. Regressive expatiation, repetition, and illustrations through example and metaphors are possible in an oral presentation with fewer problems of rhetorical discursiveness than in written presentations. A well-prepared lecturer who has flexible control of her/his discipline can make meaningful digressions which contribute to the development of his thesis topic(s). For the budding scholar, these rhetorical devices are helpful because the more ways in which ideas are cast, the greater are the chances for mentally storing and later retrieving them.

3. In a multiplicity of nonverbal signals and through a variety of body-language gestures, which college students are adept at giving, the lecturer receives instant feedback as to the clarity and effectiveness of his communication. The lecturing professor can immediately revise or recast his presentation by using the techniques in numbers 1 and 2 above. Needless to say, instant adaptations of this nature are beyond the scope of a printed text.

4. The professor who renders his lectures with vigor and finesse in precisely articulated, masterful displays of the thorough knowledge of his discipline represents the mythic model for many students of the learned college teacher. Whether or not the role of the contemporary college teacher should change from this legendary one is moot, however. Even today, many college students of all

levels of ability report that they receive both inspiration and motivation from the prototype professor-lecturer (Nelson and Scott, 1974).

In an essay on the arts of teaching and of being taught, Mark van Doren (1959) recounts the story of Socrates' disaffection with the Sophists. Socrates is reported as having become critical of the motives and worth of the Sophists because of their unwillingness to interact with their students, and their preference for lecturing principally in catchwords, slogans, platitudes, and cliches with excessive redundancy. Socrates preferred an instructional system that was antithetical to sophistry. Socratic teaching and learning were based on sustained, probing questioning of both abstruse and commonly accepted beliefs and information. Only through answering questions from any and all sources, Socrates believed, and sharing the clarified views could man ever hope to reach true wisdom.

As we turn now to a discussion of the limitations of the lecture method as the principal instructional strategy in contemporary private-traditional American colleges, we find that Socrates' ancient criticism of the lecture method still obtains. In addition, the following negative aspects of the lecture method may be cited:

1. Because of the transience of the spoken word, ideas received in a lecture prove to be very evanescent. Research has shown that rarely is more than forty-two percent of the principal ideas retained even for an hour following a lecture, and that as small an amount as seventeen percent is retrievable after a week. (See McLeish, 1968.)

2. The role of the learner during a lecture is that of a receiver. This passive role has been shown to be less productive than an active role in comparative studies of instructional systems. Active involvement in learning enhances the students' interest, attention-span, perseverance, and chaining for recall. (See Scandura, 1977.)

3. The conventional physical setting for a lecture—a group of students in various numbers, with the professor in the front and the students in rows looking at the backs of their classmates—is a distracting and enervating environment for many students. Even in lectures where the students are exemplary in conduct, the normal shiftings, breathing, coughing, and other slightly restive behavior of *homo sapiens* are found by some students to be impediments to concentration.

4. Listening, the ability to translate sound into meaning, is quantitatively the most used of the language arts and yet is the most neglected verbal communication skill in American education. This process of giving active, conscious attention to verbal sound sequences for purposes of comprehending and interpreting requires different levels of skills which can be developed. (See Butler and Jacoby, 1965, and Pauk, 1974.) The lecture method demands mature listening proficiency; unfortunately, a dearth of American students are prepared to exercise effective listening processes.

The widely diverse student populations in contemporary American colleges generally do not possess the requisite tools for learning which our private-traditional colleges expect. The lecture method, which continues to be the core instructional strategy in these institutions, fails to meet the learning needs of substantially large numbers of the students. Within the past ten years, however, even private-traditional colleges have begun some exploratory efforts to engage students in a new relationship in the teaching-learning process. These initial shifts away from traditional didactic instruction, which will be discussed in chapter five, include reviews of exemplary teaching that utilize diagnostic/prescriptive and individualized/personalized practices. Permeating these new, prototype strategies is a philosophy of holistic, pluralistic education and belief in the productivity of andragogy in college teaching, which will be discussed, also, in the next chapter.

Land-Grant-State College Instruction

Clark Kerr (1964) has characterized the last quarter of the nineteenth century as the period of the first major transformation in American higher education. He attributed to the Morrill Acts the land-grant college bills which were passed in 1862 and 1890 by the Congress of the United States, the principal leverage in changing the classical curriculum of traditional American higher education of that day. Accepting the legitimacy of teaching agriculture and applied sciences in land-grant colleges reshaped the mission and role of postsecondary education in America. And these changes may be viewed as the university's natural responses to expanding societal values brought about through a realigning of the academic, vocational, economic, and industrial needs of that time.

The fact that the land-grant colleges did not exclude the traditional college curriculum but added agriculture and the mechanical arts into a broadened higher educational curriculum is perceived by K. Patricia Cross (1976) as one of the great success stories in American education. It is her belief that the Morrill Acts changed more than the curriculum of colleges; they changed the very posture of American higher education. They moved the college from a preoccupation with isolated scholarship to active involvement in the life of the society through applied research, extension, and instruction of the offsprings of the working classes.

Developing as they did some two hundred years after the prestigious, private American colleges, the land-grant-state colleges have always had an identity problem. And even today, many of these institutions are involved in analytical dialogues concerning their mission and function. Frederic Heimberger (1964) and Brubacher and Rudy (1976) believe that the satisfactory resolution of this central dilemma is critical to the future growth, development, and service of land-grant colleges. Clearly meeting the challenge of their multiple functions with creative programs is especially important for these institutions at this point in time, for the major burden of educating contemporary new-type college students rests upon them even as it did in the past.

When the first Morrill Act established land-grant colleges in 1862 to teach agricultural and mechanical courses, nontraditional students began to matriculate from previously untapped and unsolicited strata of American society. From the very outset, therefore, land-grant colleges confronted problems of developing a federally mandated curriculum that differed from those in private-traditional institutions and of meeting the learning needs of students who were seriously underprepared for higher education. It must not be forgotten that free, tax-supported high schools in several states did not become a fact of life until after the Kalamazoo decision in 1872. College-preparatory departments, therefore, were a conventional adjunct to many midwestern and central plains land-grant colleges during the nineteenth century. (See Brubacher and Rudy, 1976.)

The second Morrill Act in 1890 increased federal aid to land-grant and state colleges for implementing programs in applied sciences and mechanical arts. In essence, a new dimension in the concept of higher education was mandated by the Congress of the United States for "all of the children of all of the people" which sharply differed from European and Ivy League-type American colleges. Land-grant-state colleges may be considered as truly indigenous, unique American institutions of learning. Their multipurpose programs of study, which blend liberal arts programs with those in engineering, agriculture, and applied sciences, attempt to meet the diverse interests and needs of a pluralistic society and the abilities of the heterogeneous student populations who enroll in them.

The instructional systems of land-grant-state institutions reflect their multiple purposes and functions and they vary markedly in type and quality. Those institutions which remain strongly committed to their limited nineteenth century concerns continue to focus upon agricultural and vocational studies through laboratory, demonstration, field-work, internships, extension, and practicum approaches to learning augmented with few liberal arts studies. On the other hand, those land-grant-state institutions that have moved far beyond any concept of restricted mission or purpose have extended their range of interests and have surpassed some of the most distinguished private, traditional-élite colleges in our country. Needless to say, in the latter may be found a veritable constellation of instructional systems which respond to student and program diversity.

It is no secret that in some of the renowned land-grant-state institutions of higher education (especially in the "Big Ten"), sustained ideological controversy has existed between their colleges and/or divisions of arts and sciences and those of the agricultural, engineering, and applied sciences. On the one hand, the arts and sciences faculties espouse élite-traditional values in admissions criteria, faculty standards, instruction, curriculum, and academic standards; while on the other hand, the agricultural-engineering-applied sciences divisions have promulgated various accommodations to the reality of student heterogeneity and the real-life vocational demands of the greater society. Deep differences of opinion on questions of educational goals and standards are reflected, therefore, in instructional emphases and strategies in land-grant-state institutions. (See Heimberger, 1964.)

Even as it is used as the principal instructional tool in private-traditional institutions, the lecture method is used in colleges and divisions of arts and sciences in land-grant-state institutions of higher education. The positive and negative aspects of the lecture method as presented in an earlier section of this chapter apply to its exercise in land-grant colleges. Thus, it is probable that the most effective teaching-learning procedures in land-grant-state institutions occur in the agricultural-engineering-applied sciences divisions. The purposes of these fields are clearly designated and the vocational relationship of the course work is easily identifiable.

Frank Lloyd Wright's notable contributions to architecture are customarily attributed to his application of the dogma that "form follows function." In the field of education as well as in architecture, when a discipline has decided upon identifiable goals and purposes, it then becomes relatively easy to activate the necessary methodologies to attain them. In land-grant-state institutions of higher education, the fields of agriculture, engineering, and the applied sciences have clearly identifiable goals to which the courses of studies relate directly. These studies usually involve considerable student activity in the laboratory, or in field, apprenticeship, work-study, demonstration, or internship programs. Both on and off the campus, these various types of hands-on, direct-exposure learning experiences contribute largely to the attainment of course and student objectives. The instructional systems in these fields of study, therefore, generally meet the needs of the heterogeneous student populations in land-grant-state institutions with greater success than do studies in the arts and sciences disciplines in these colleges.

Black College Instruction

The higher educational institutions in the United States that predominantly enroll black students have a history that is inextricably interwoven with the circumstances of slavery in America, the abolition movement, the Civil War, emancipation of the slaves and the reconstruction period, the Industrial Revolution, the Morrill Acts of 1862 and 1890, American Home Mission Societies, the Plessy *vs*. Ferguson decision in 1896, and the civil rights movement in the 1950s. Prior to the 1960s these institutions were customarily called "Negro colleges." They were established because of stringent policies of segregation of blacks in education, religion, and other social institutions in the states of the old South, and to a lesser extent in the border states and elsewhere. (See Robert R. Moton Memorial Institute, 1974.)

Barely 12 of the 120 black colleges and universities are more than 100 years old, but during their period of existence they have provided postsecondary education to the overwhelming majority of America's blacks. These institutions, nonetheless, have never been sufficiently financed, staffed, or had adequate academic resources, although they were ostensibly operating under the doctrine of "separate but equal."

Sixteen of the thirty-four traditionally black public institutions of higher learning are land-grant institutions. Yet even these institutions have never been financed as adequately as their counterpart for white students. Operating under these serious economic restrictions, nevertheless, black colleges and universities have had to provide higher education for the most seriously academically disadvantaged segment of American society. (See McGee, 1977.)

The instructional systems of black colleges have been from the very first marked by extreme diversity. In their early mission, being responsible for educating former slaves who were hampered by having no previous legal access to any formal education, these black institutions had to be concerned frequently with elementary and secondary education as well as with postsecondary studies. Most black colleges, therefore, did not truly become institutions for postsecondary education until the first and second decades of the twentieth century. (See Mayhew, 1973.)

From the outset, the curricula of black colleges focused upon the pragmatic needs of their students. Thus in the nineteenth century most of these colleges primarily offered courses in agriculture, manual and mechanic arts, homemaking, teacher-preparation, and theology. Undergirding the foregoing curricula were basic skills education courses in an academy or preparatory department. The traditional liberal arts were not comprehensively offered except in four or five of the black institutions prior to the 1940s. (See Hamilton, 1977.)

Martha Maxwell (1979) has recently echoed a question that has been raised frequently in the past: By what means has it been possible for black colleges to stimulate effective learning in a student population that frequently enrolls in college with impeding academic deficits, due to segregated and inferior elementary and secondary education? Granted that substantial numbers of students in black colleges have not been adequately educated to levels of single-standard, competitive efficiency in the total American society, still, how was it possible to guide the development of even a significant few under such adverse circumstances? What factors in these institutions increased black students' invulnerability to their impoverished backgrounds? What factors enhanced their repertory of coping behaviors for unknown societal encounters? And through what means were they "turned on"—i.e., given senses of personhood and mission?

Benjamin Mays (1971), Samuel D. Proctor (1978), Charles V. Willie and Chester M. Hedgepeth, Jr. (1979), and Kenneth B. Clark (1979), among others, have addressed the question of valid academic attainment in black colleges by black students through analyzing the nature of the educational programs in these institutions. In their writings may be found a common core of basic assumptions that they perceive black colleges through the years have incorporated as integral commitments upon which to rest the totality of their educational endeavors.

It must be noted at this point that the philosophical guides that follow ideally should undergird all higher educational studies in America (and for that matter, the lower levels of public education, also). These beliefs touch at the very heart of the essential humanizing elements of the educative process. Unfortunately, in all too many instances, American education on all levels has drifted and crystallized into obsolescent curriculum rigidities and normative homogenizations of student achievement standards.

At their best, American black institutions of higher education are committed consciously to the following premises:

1. *Belief in the random distribution of "talent" in the family of man.* (Thus, in spite of their academic entry-level status, students are genuinely welcomed, accepted, and encouraged to strive for the attainment of their unique interests and dreams. They are encouraged to understand that only when a human being becomes motivated and commits himself to the attainment of a goal is it possible to ascertain the quality of his developmental potential.)

2. *Belief in the power of an individual to transcend environmental impediments.* (The transcendence of the affective nature of man over his cognitive and physical ones is conscientiously espoused. Students are guided in understanding that the very essence of their humanity is being able to "call forth more"—in being able to persist in the face of adversity.)

3. *Belief in the necessity for and the responsibility of an enlightened individual to "pass on his light."* (An intrinsic element in teaching academically disadvantaged students involves "infecting," "igniting," and inspiring them through example. Thus, an instructor who is vigorously and genuinely enthusiastic about his discipline, and who shares his unique personal perceptions of issues and problems in connection with his cognitive expatiations tends to "turn-on" students through personalizing instruction. In turn, students' thoughtful, personal assessments and views are encouraged and shared. The central lesson to be learned in the foregoing is that no single person [including the textbook-person] has total, comprehensive perception of any issue or problem.)

4. *Belief in the efficacy of facing the reality of human generality,*

uniqueness, limitations, and strengths without cynicism, posturing, or subterfuge while living in two worlds simultaneously—one black, one white. (The advantages and disadvantages of seeking personal identity in a pluralistic, technological, racist society are explored in different ways. Whether within the confines of regular course study or in informal, cocurricular settings, students receive understanding assistance in coming to terms with the duality of being a black minority member as well as an American citizen. Black institutions stress multiethnic perceptions of humanity and reality, and assist students in learning to cope with the various roles expected of them in the American *Zeitgeist* and *Weltanschauung*.)

The foregoing philosophical guides have been called "humanistic" by some educators and "moralistic" by others. Be that as it may, black leaders in America who are the products of black higher educational institutions generally attribute their noteworthy attainment to the continual (almost evangelical) attention given in these institutions to the nurturing of students' personal perspectives and attitudes along with their cognitive development. A case in point is a moving testament of Samuel D. Proctor (1978) in which he evocatively presents the multiple levels of intellectual and affective stimulation and development which he experienced at Virginia Union University as a callow youth from the segregated schools of Norfolk, Virginia.

While on the one hand agreeing with the importance and the necessity of black colleges being strongly committed to nurturing the development of their students' personal identities and life perspectives, Kenneth B. Clark (1979) warns that black colleges must face the challenge of their frequent production of students who cannot compete in the single-standard marketplace of our society. In fact, Clark bluntly suggests, many black colleges even today are conferring "second-class," racially determined, "double-standard" degrees. Except for a very few exceptional students, Clark argues, black colleges must face-up to the impossibility of most students compensating for twelve years of underpreparation in inferior public schools *while at the same time* pursuing baccalaureate studies. What is needed, he suggests, is for black colleges to engage in a drastic reexamination and reorganization of the traditional four-year limit college format. The contemporary black college, he believes, must be changed into a realistic structure in which students' high-level, competitive attainment is the rule and not the exception.

Community College Instruction

In 1964 Clark Kerr predicted that in the foreseeable future foreign models for American universities would no longer obtain. Kerr reasoned that the distinctive, pluralistic way of life in the United States would eventually require a unique, particular type of higher educational structure to serve the special needs of American citizens. The establishment of land-grant-state colleges and universities in the late nineteenth century is considered by Kerr and others as the beginning of the transformation of American higher education into a truly new-world structure. And the incredibly rapid development of community and junior colleges since 1960, in response to expanding intellectual needs of American industry, government, and other societal segments, may be considered to be the nucleus of the second significant transformation in American higher education.

In 1960, according to the American Association of Community and Junior Colleges (AACJC), 600,000 students were enrolled in some 678 community and junior colleges. By 1979, more than four and a half million students attended some 1,500 of these institutions, and these students' precollege academic underpreparation and impeding sociocultural factors relegate the vast majority of them to the high-risk category. (See Friedmand and Thompson, 1970; Mulka and Sheerin, 1974; and Gordon, 1975.) Today, in the United States, there are more two-year institutions of higher education than four-year institutions. And just eight years ago Karabel (1973) found that in excess of one-third of all enrollees in four-year institutions had entered by way of a community or junior college. Inasmuch as community and junior colleges are overwhelmingly public, free, tax-supported, and open admissions institutions, they have become virtually the thirteenth and fourteenth years in the American "common-school" system.

Grant and Hoeber (1978) report that community and junior colleges pride themselves on being "teaching colleges," i.e., their primary concern is classroom teaching, with only secondary importance, if any, placed on research outside the classroom. Without apology, these institutions view research not as an end in itself nor as means to advance an instructor's career, but as a means to improve the quality and productivity of education at their particular institution. It is not surprising, therefore, that community and junior colleges are today both the bellwethers and arbiters of innovative instructional programs for high-risk college students.

K. Patricia Cross (1976, p. 10) reports that community and junior colleges are perceived by traditional college faculties as being in essence "buffer zones." This dubious designation probably emerged because the *sine qua non* of the instructional systems in community and junior colleges is a "basic skills program." In skills development programs, these colleges attempt to guide the high-risk students' development of the essential tools-for-learning in higher education that their entry-level examinations and secondary school records indicated that they lack.

The focus, quantity, and quality of basic skills instruction, as well as the principal instructional systems utilized in community and junior colleges, depend to a great extent upon the particular mission or purpose of the college. Some of these institutuions are two-year technical institutes, and others are "feeder" satellite "lower-level" campuses for the central university, and function for it as "general education," screening, or preparatory branches; still others are primarily bastions of adult, continuing, and "life-long" education.

The general education curriculum in community and junior colleges for the most part is similar to that found in traditional private and land-grant-state institutions—the exploratory study of the humanities, natural sciences, and social sciences. In these areas of study, all too frequently the lecture method dominates as the sole instructional delivery-system, even as it does in traditional colleges. And inasmuch as student progress and tenure in general education courses are intimately related to students' entry-level proficiencies, attrition is very high in these areas of study for high-risk students. Cross (1976) reports that, in many community and junior colleges, faculty members have little understanding of the academic status of high-risk students, and thus they make little effort to provide meaningful instruction which is commensurate with their limited academic capabilities.

In the most comprehensive survey and analysis to date of basic skills programs in two- and four-year institutions of higher education, L. L. Sullivan (1978) reports that some very promising instructional strategies are incorporated in them. Despite the fact that basic skills programs function under an array of organizational titles—"learning center," "academic reinforcement," "developmental studies," "remedial-compensatory program," "learning assistance program," and many others—at their best, the premises that follow are evident:

1. Inasmuch as high-risk students are admitted, the college is philosophically and financially committed to meeting the educa-

tional needs of these students through a broad spectrum of ongoing academic support services.

2. The delivery systems for the academic support services are flexible and multi-faceted and provide for: (a) guided learning in various class-size groupings (one-to-one, small, large) as the nature of the subject and the objectives dictate; (b) autoinstruction and self-paced learning; (c) multimedia and multimodal independent study; (d) course objectives that relate to students' immediate and future goals; and (e) a focus upon broad meanings rather than fragmented information through explication, illustration, and interpretation.

3. Learning-to-learn skills which have immediate transferability to students' academic study in other college courses constitute the core of basic skills programs. The developmental studies that enhance verbal proficiency, mathematics, and study skills, therefore, are specifically linked to students' college disciplines.

4. Basic skills faculty members are sensitive to the uniqueness of human individuality and understand the relationships between cognitive and affective development. Every effort is made to involve students in identifying the personal relevance of a course to his unique goals and objectives. And the experiential resources of students are regularly utilized in the ongoing classroom interactions.

5. Synergetic principles dominate the relationships between diagnosed student needs, prescribed programs of learning, the materials of instruction, and the evaluation of outcomes, and the essential linkages between these elements are evident.

6. The students are viewed as adults, and as such, principles of andragogy (not pedagogy) are emphasized. In this regard, students are treated as being mature, needs-oriented, autonomous individuals, and their learning is facilitated in psychologically supportive milieus.

In sum, basic skills programs in community and junior colleges, at their best, face the reality of student populations that need additional and continuing assistance in pursuing the types of learning activities required in American higher education. In this regard, therefore, these programs represent a clearly defined break with didactic, optionless, conventional patterns of higher educational instruction.

Summary

The instructional systems in American higher education tend to reflect, on the one hand, the historical European roots of many institutions, and on the other hand, uniquely specialized American educational purposes and functions. In private-traditional colleges, which are strongly based on European university models, the philosophy of instruction continues to be generally grounded in didacticism. And in such settings, the lecture is the overwhelming instructional mode.

Because of their multiple purposes and functions, land-grant-state colleges and universities reflect a variety of traditional and pragmatic instructional strategies. It is not unreasonable to use the terms *hybrid* and *potpourri* in reference to the diverse systems of instruction in land-grant-state institutions.

Black and community colleges may be considered as the most indigenously American institutions of higher education. Emerging as they have in response to special demands in the society to meet the needs of particular student populations, these institutions have incorporated highly adaptive instructional systems.

The elements in the instructional systems of private-traditional, land-grant-state, black, and community colleges which have adaptive and adoptive contributions to make to an instructional paradigm for high-risk students will be presented in chapter four.

Chapter 4

AN INSTRUCTIONAL PARADIGM FOR HIGH-RISK COLLEGE STUDENTS

Introduction

In earlier sections of this monograph a framework of reference for this chapter was developed. Significant factors were discussed which impinge upon the raison d'etre of an instructional paradigm for high-risk college students: the role of paradigms and the nature of instructional systems design; various perceptions of the post-1960 college enrollment boom; the characteristics of high-risk students; and descriptions and assessments of instructional systems in American higher educational institutions—private-traditional, land-grant state, black, and community. These factors, in conjunction with post-World War II societal forces, which have generated unprecedented changes in the American way of life, are the matrix of the need today for reconstructive instructional practices in higher education.

Before presenting the paradigm for instructing high-risk college students, let us discuss briefly the substantial past history of accommodation in American higher education to student diversity. Contrary to popular belief, academic support for underprepared college entrants is not a phenomenon of the post-1960 years. Indeed, there are segments of the higher educational community who argue persuasively that contemporary American collegians differ only in quantitative terms and not in qualitative ways from earlier student populations.

Brubacher and Rudy (1976) present the following significant milestones in the history of educational adjustments to student heterogeneity in American colleges and universities:

1. In 1852, President Henry P. Tappan of the University of Michigan in his inaugural address decried the dilution of course content in colleges in order to meet the needs of poorly prepared students.
2. In 1869, the launching of the elective system at Harvard by President Charles W. Eliot broke the former lock-step of totally prescribed college curricula. (The elective system is in essence an attempt to make the college curriculum relevant and meaningful to the diverse interests of undergraduate students.) Students for the first time were allowed to choose studies for their intrinsic rather than their disciplinary value and to satisfy their personal predilections.
3. In 1874, Harvard began to offer a simplified, fundamental course in freshman English at the request of the faculty who were concerned about the unsatisfactory writing skills of many new-entrants.
4. In 1890, the College Entrance Examination Board was founded as an attempt to standardize admissions requirements in response to general college dissatisfaction with the inadequacies of new entrants.
5. In 1894, Wellesley College offered a course for freshmen who were in need of increased, general academic college preparation.
6. By 1915, 350 colleges in the U.S.A. reported to the U.S. commissioner of education that their institutions had college preparatory departments, academies, or high schools directly connected with them. New entrants who were academically deficient frequently had to attend the "preparatory" adjunct to the college for one or two years. (As late as 1894 such students comprised forty percent of the entering students in American colleges.)

The milestones cited above in various ways attest to the fact that American colleges have accepted for a considerable period of time responsibility for helping students overcome impeding weaknesses in academic background and skills. And whether in the nineteenth century or today, academic support programs have a variety of philosophical orientations and organizational patterns. To a large extent, the program diversity is a natural reflection of the differences in purposes, organization, and clientele of American higher education.

K. Patricia Cross (1976) has traced identifiable changes from the nineteenth century onward in the predominant concerns and foci in American college academic support programs. For the most part, the flow has been from isolated, narrowly conceived, poorly funded efforts to integrated, broadly-conceptualized, regularly budgeted programs. Prior to the 1940s, the academic support programs were largely one-shot how-to-study courses. These early programs were developed in response to a rather simplistic perception of the cause(s) of ineffective educational performance. Since many of the students in need of the tools for college study came from "good families," the colleges attributed their inadequacies, not to lack of ability, but to immaturity and lack of self-discipline in organizing and utilizing college-type study habits.

Beginning in the 1940s, Cross identifies the addition of remedial reading to the how-to-study courses for underprepared college students. This new emphasis on reading deficiencies may be viewed as a spin-off from the general focus on standardized testing on all levels of American public education in the late 1930s and early 1940s, and increased awareness in the society of academic standards and achievement. Remedial reading as well as the how-to-study courses were customarily voluntary and non-credit and were usually conducted by counselors or other student-personnel workers. Some of these courses were offered during summer sessions prior to the freshman year. It should be noted that the inclusion of remedial reading instruction for low-achieving college students in the 1940s marked a broadened perception of the problems of high-risk students and an awakening sensitivity to the importance of the tools-of-learning in college study.

In the late 1950s and early 1960s, increased understanding developed of the true dimensions of the post-World War II college enrollment boom. Various analyses of the personal, demographic, and academic characteristics and traits of these newcomers to higher education revealed the great extent of their diversity and heterogeneity. In light of this broadened perception of high-risk students, institutions of higher education at this time began to develop programs for their underprepared enrollees which included services and studies that went beyond the formerly purely academic concerns. Undergirding these new programs was increased sensitivity to the possible contribution of psycho- and sociocultural factors to academic effectiveness.

Cross notes that in the late 1950s and early 1960s many colleges began to differentiate between so-called "low-ability" students (i.e., those who had very low percentile ranks on I.Q. and/or psychological tests of intellectual potential) and so-called "underachievers" (those students who had acceptable I.Q. and/or learning-potential scores, but who had unacceptable high school academic records and/or poor achievement test scores). As a natural outgrowth of these categorizations, colleges and universities began to provide counseling and personal motivational activities to address student problems which were newly perceived as being related to academic achievement. Contemporary research on the learning styles of high-risk students as well as studies concerning their self-concepts, levels of aspiration, and role models all made significant contributions to the development at this time of academic support programs in American institutions of higher education. The so-called "low-ability" students generally were unprovided for in even these broadened-purposes programs, however, and they rarely survived two semesters in college. On the other hand, salvaging "underachievers" was the principal concern through the 1960s in academic support programs in American higher education.

In the late 1960s and into the 1970s, as "all of the children of all of the people" began to enroll in college, the full dimensions of academic, personal, and cultural differences in our pluralistic student bodies were finally acknowledged and generally accepted by higher education administrations. Thus factors associated with sociocultural differences in aspiration, career choices, and attitudes toward intellectual development were beginning to be diagnosed and planned for in academic support programs. And as the 1980s dawn, American higher education is beginning to comprehend fully the infinite complexity of academic underpreparation and performance and the variety of services which this complexity requires. It is becoming increasingly obvious that effective academic support services for today's high-risk populations must provide not only pragmatic, individualized basic skills development, but also ongoing personalized cognitive, social, and affective development. Piecemeal, band-aid approaches are inadequate and can be countenanced no longer.

The multi-faceted instructional system for high-risk students in contemporary American colleges which is presented in this chapter is an amalgam of theoretical and pragmatic teaching-learning strategies. In an effort to accommodate the intellectual and personal diversity of the students, the methodologies are designed to be as varied as the clients' heterogeneity. And in this future-shock world in which societal values and customs as well as knowledge and technologies are evanescent and become obsolescent within a college generation, the instructional system herein presented focuses upon the overall applicability and transferability of learning activities to immediate and future situations alike. The means and processes of the instructional system have, therefore, a coordinate relationship to the designated ends or products.

The Why: *Purposes, Mission, Role, Goals*

Chapter one presented a definition of an instructional system, and stressed that in an effective system a synergetic relationship exists between the purposes, goals, objectives, content, methods, materials-of-instruction, and the evaluation. Additionally, in the discussion of the pivotal role of the *why*-component of an instructional system, the point was made that it is the *sine qua non* upon which all contributing elements of the system rest. Daniel Clowes (1979) subscribes to this view of the importance of a clearly defined purpose, and he affirms that indeed it is fruitless to try to establish the *form* of an instructional program without first developing and adopting the program's *function*. Belaboring this vital point further, there is merit in saying that the "whyness" of an instructional system is the foundation of its "whatness," "howness," and "how-wellness." And indeed, by borrowing the theme of the modern architectural revolution it may be said that "form should follow function."

The point to be stressed about the effects of the student enrollment boom in the 1960s upon American institutions of higher education is this: *the extension within the past two decades of equality of educational opportunity to segments of the population who were previously not considered to be "college material" must be understood to be the primary force and reason for the development of alternative programs and services in higher education.* And it must not be forgotten that accompanying increased ease in the accessibility of postsecondary education are problems of providing *quality* as well as *equality* of education. The full force of John Gardner's plaintive query in 1961—"Can we be equal and excellent too?"—truly put American higher education on the horns of the dilemma.

Courses and programs for high-risk college students gain their definition and direction from, and rest upon, clearly stipulated and articulated purposes. The development of these program purposes by an institution of higher education, however, of necessity is a highly individual, internal matter. Each program must be designed to serve the diagnosed needs of a particular student body, and must be intimately related to the central mission of each college or university. The variegated nature of admissions policies, programs of study, academic standards, and philosophies of education in American institutions of higher education cannot but indicate the need for great diversity in their instructional systems.

In spite of the need for uniqueness in the stated purposes of different instructional systems for high-risk students, there are some common elements basic to the development of any institution's program. These key design decisions should be made by the institution on the basis of the anticipated function of its program to the end that there is the desired synergetic relationship between function and the form (organization, courses, standards, etc.) of the program. Fundamental to arriving at a statement of the purpose(s) of a program for high-risk students is the institution's development of consensus on the following matters:

1. Will the philosophical orientation of the program be *remedial*, *compensatory*, or *developmental*?
2. Shall the program be a *threshold* (i.e., preparatory, transitional) one or a support (i.e., ongoing, mainstream-related) effort?

In the ensuing sections, the writer will present some significant observations on the preceding questions which provided background for decision-making about the purposes of this instructional system for high-risk college students.

1. A REMEDIAL, COMPENSATORY, OR DEVELOPMENTAL FOCUS?

In making this first, critical decision about the philosophical focus of the instructional program, it should be borne in mind that the terms *remedial*, *compensatory*, and *developmental* are frequently used interchangeably in the literature and in actual practice and generate considerable semantic and ideological controversy. In the 1970s, largely through the research and analyses of Roueche and Kirk (1973), Miller and Gordon (1974), Cross (1976), and Levine (1979), the three terms are used now with increased specificity and have become more precisely defined. *Remedial* is generally considered to be the most negative of the three and implies the student's "deficit status" that must be "corrected" before he is "ready" to enter certain programs of study. *Compensatory* is still frequently used synonymously with "remedial," and, in addition to implying the need for correcting disabilities, implies also the need for overcoming past deprivations and sociocultural disadvantages. *Developmental,* the most recently devised term of the three, is generally conceived as the most positive: it emphasizes the building of new strengths and the enhancement of skills and attitudes, and studiously avoids directing the principal energies of the program upon student weaknesses.

It is the position in this paradigm that there is a place in the stated purposes of a comprehensive instructional system for high-risk students for each of the three philosophical orientations. *It does not have to be an "either-or" decision; it can be a "both-and" amalgam.* Prerequisite skills can be purposed to be remediated in an atmosphere of restitution in conjunction with the development of new coping skills. And it will be shown later that all three terms may be accommodated under an umbrella term, *pluralistic.*

2. A THRESHOLD OR SUPPORT PROGRAM?

Implicit in the decision relating to whether the instructional system will be essentially *threshold* or *support* in nature are accompanying decisions about (a) the administrative locus and aegis of the program, (b) dimensions of the learning objectives, (c) length of student tenure in the program, (d) whether student participation will be mandatory or personally discretionary, and (e) if the courses of study accrue credit or not.

The term *threshold* is used metaphorically to indicate that the program of studies is initial, prefatorial, adjunctive, and transitional in nature and must be "negotiated" satisfactorily by high-risk students prior to entering into "mainstream" college studies. Threshold instructional systems generally are (1) freshman programs of one or two semesters in duration, which are frequently preceded by a "pre-college summer," and may occasionally be organized in the form of a two-year "College of General Studies"; (2) operate under the aegis of the institution's offices of Student Personnel, the vice-president for academic affairs, or even the dean of the College of Arts and Sciences as a semiseparate, adjunctive unit to the main undergraduate college; (3) have limited objectives—frequently focusing only on basic skills and learning-to-learn skills; and (4) strive to maintain a climate for learning which is universally *protective, supportive, motivational,* and *emboldening.*

Support programs, on the other hand, (1) recognize the implausibility of overcoming long-established, precollege academic inadequacies in short-term, limited-objectives programs that are separated from the mainstream college; (2) offer ongoing academic reinforcement throughout the entire undergraduate curriculum wherever needed—in general education, prerequisite skills, major and minor sequences; (3) provide a multiplicity of academic support services and instructional strategies such as tutoring, *ad hoc* problems-institutes, computer-assisted instruction as well as autoinstructional programs, and self-paced modular instruction; and (4) involve the total faculty in various ways as working partners in the program.

A continuing controversy relating to the development of the purposes for either threshold or support instructional programs concerns whether the programs should require student participation to be mandatory or discretionary. Equally controversial are decisions concerning the giving of academic course credit for studies which are not truly postsecondary in nature. Increasingly within the late 1970s a strong case has been made for mandatory student participation in an instructional system which provides both threshold and support services, and transcript credit (*i.e.*, credit which is nonattributable to graduation requirements) for the courses of study.

The case for mandatory student participation in credit-giving courses includes the following principal arguments:

1. An institution of higher education committed to the philosophy of equality of educational opportunity *ipso facto* espouses the mandatory upgrading of student underpreparation through any and all appropriate academic services. Not only would initially diagnosed academic needs be addressed in threshold programs, but also ongoing academic support would be available to decrease the likelihood of the open door becoming a revolving door.

2. By giving transcript credit for courses of study successfully attended, the institution recognizes and values student effort in making a positive effort to overcome underpreparation.

3. Mandatory, credit-bearing programs for high-risk students clearly signal the institution's direct commitment to student heterogeneity and the need for academic diversity.

THE *WHY* PARADIGM: CONCLUSION

It is proposed in this paradigm that inasmuch as the purposes, mission, and goal of an instructional system for high-risk college students radiate from the institution's uncompromising commitment to both equality of educational opportunity and quality of education for all enrollees, it follows that reasons for the existence of a non-traditional program of studies would be validated maximally through: (1) a synthesis of the philosophical orientations of remedial, compensatory, and developmental teaching/learning strategies; (2) an incremental continuum of both threshold and support instructional approaches; and (3) mandatory student participation in transcript credit programs of study.

Thus by broadly purposing to render multiple academic and personal educational services to all students who need to increase their proficiencies, the inherent meaning of equal educational opportunity becomes a reality.

The What: *Curriculum (Learning Objectives and Courses of Study)*

In earlier sections of this chapter the synergetic interrelatedness of the *why, what, how,* and *how well* of an instructional system was discussed. Of particular importance to this section about the curriculum, however, is the basic connection between the recognized need for a special instructional program for high-risk students and what the content of such a program encompasses. In this regard, the point may be made that the curriculum is essentially a translation into a practical, empirical form or structure of the premises for the existence of the system.

The nature of the curriculum for an instructional system for highrisk college students is predicated upon, and embedded in, the quality of the precollege educational experiences of the students. Prior sections of this monograph focused upon the history of inadequate and inappropriate precollege preparation in the United States for traditional higher educational studies. It should be reiterated, therefore, that underpreparation for college study is not a phenomenon peculiar to the late twentieth century in the United States of America. American institutions of higher education have never enjoyed in large numbers the academic products of such secondary schools as the European *lycées* and *Gymnasiums,* or students who have had an Etonian or Harrow-type precollege preparation. Insufficient mastery of the "tools-of-learning" (basic mathematical, verbal, and study skills that facilitate independent, postsecondary learning) has been the rule rather than the exception in American college entrants. The "tools-of-learning" have become, therefore, the nucleus of the curriculum in the threshold program for high-risk students.

In addition to precollege underpreparation in the tools-of-learning, high-risk college entrants for the past fifteen years revealed inadequate mastery of the "basic knowledge" on the CEEB Achievement Tests. This knowledge is generally considered to be prerequisite to effective study in the conventional college disciplines—the natural sciences, social sciences, and the humanities. It is for this reason that some institutions of higher education include introductory, survey courses in these disciplines as a significant part of the curriculum in their instructional system for high-risk students. (Levine, 1979)

In some institutions, "basic knowledge" courses for high-risk students are categorized as "general education" in the threshold curriculum. They are a blend of an introduction to the area of study, a general overview, and a compressed survey of material which should have been mastered in precollege studies. Partially due to the different and occasionally conflicting definitions and purposes attributed to general education, and partially because of problems associated with faculty selection for them, "basic knowledge" courses associated with programs for high-risk students remain a highly controversial matter. And in this paradigm, basic knowledge courses will not be included in the "threshold" curriculum as an integral part of the program of studies. Later sections of this chapter, and chapter five, will present techniques for gradually mainstreaming high-risk students in basic knowledge courses through ongoing support services.

Upgrading and/or developing the cognitive and affective tools-of-learning is the highest priority curriculum concern in this paradigm, even as it is in the vast majority of extant instructional systems for high-risk students. In spite of the fact that there is no commonly accepted categorization of these "tools," increasingly the literature reports the following classification:

1. *Basic Skills*

   Mathematics—customarily including arithmetical computations with integers, fractions, decimals, and percents; fundamental algebra through quadratic equations; and fundamental geometry.
   English Language Study—customarily including the improve-

ment and/or development of the mechanics of English usage, vocabulary, listening, and reading for ideas as the bases of writing ideas in paragraphs, and the embedding of paragraphs in a coherent composition.

2. *Learning-to-Learn Skills*

Orientation to Higher Education—introduction to the history, structure, purposes, and goals of various types of postsecondary education in general, and the students' own college in particular.

Study Skills—the development of strategies for organizing for study and a repertory of methods and techniques of study appropriate to the students' academic pursuits.

Personal Development: College, Career, and Life Planning —increasing students' conscious involvement in their personal and intellectual development; stimulating the examination of personal interests, purposes, goals; guiding and counseling the development of appropriate plans and actions for resolving impediments to attaining individual objectives.

Increasingly in the 1970s, the content in the courses of study for high-risk students is organized in "performance objectives." (Other terms which are currently used to refer to performance objectives are: *behavioral objectives, learning objectives, operationally defined objectives, measurable objectives,* and *special instructional objectives.*) *Performance objectives* are explicit statements of what students will be able to do or how they will be expected to behave after completing a prescribed unit, module, or course of instruction. As such, they are written, verbal descriptions of specific terminal behaviors or instructional outcomes required of students to signify successful completion of their study. (Briggs, 1979)

Encapsulating course content into performance objectives has been adjudged in some institutions to be one of the more promising processes in instructional programs for high-risk students. In instructional programs that are "product-oriented" (i.e., established to secure empirical results), the explicit specification of the terminal behaviors expected after the teaching/learning interchanges provides an internal accountability mechanism. Additionally, performance objectives render the following benefits to the overall instructional effectiveness:

1. They are effective media for identifying for learning a large

range of information and skills for students who possess widely varying academic attainment.

2. They require teachers to make discrete decisions as to what skills their students should master in every teaching episode. Thus this clarification of instructional intent decreases imprecision in communication during the teaching/learning interplay.

3. They supply direct information to the students about the content and skills which they are to master. Students, therefore, do not have to "second-guess" as to the intent of the teacher, for they know exactly what they must do to demonstrate mastery. This knowledge sharply decreases wasting both time and effort.

4. They facilitate effective communication in the university-wide community about course outcomes and the overall purposes of the entire instructional system for high-risk students. Performance objectives supply a concise overview to university administrators, student advisors, faculty in other divisions, as well as to parents who desire some understanding of the legitimacy of the educational program.

In Appendix A may be found an example of the content in basic English which has been encapsulated into performance objectives. And it is the position in this paradigm that there are salient advantages in this instructional practice.

In spite of the fact that today there is some consensus regarding the areas of study in basic skills and learning-to-learn skills courses, controversy continues in many institutions of higher education about the actual range in difficulty in course content and skills that high-risk college students must master in these remedial-developmental programs. At the very heart of this issue is the question: How far back into preparatory skill development should these courses go? (How simple, how elementary, how fundamental should the content be?) And the answer to this question which is endorsed in this paradigm is one that many American institutions of higher education still find it difficult to accept: If colleges and universities admit students as legitimate members of their populations without adequate preparation for their programs of study, it is both reasonable and just that the institutions provide the requisite developmental studies. (In other words, institutions have a moral and a legal obligation, *ipso facto* the admissions validation, to change the learning skills and deficit academic sophistication of students from the levels of their initial, matriculated status.)

The majority of the content in the courses of study in instructional systems for high-risk students, therefore, may be termed appropriately, "old wine in new bottles." For indeed, the content and skills are a part of the curriculum in elementary and secondary educational programs throughout the United States. The "new bottles"—a diagnostic-prescriptive delivery-system based upon principles of individualized, personalized instruction in "compressed-time" learning modules—will be explicated in the *how* section of this chapter.

Before leaving the *what* in this instructional paradigm, however, some attention must be given briefly to the largely unresolved issue concerning the most appropriate place for reading improvement in the curriculum for high-risk students. In many institutions, reading development courses are a separate entity in the instructional program; and indeed, some high-risk instructional systems are titled "Reading/Study Skills" programs. It is the position in this paradigm, nonetheless, that the development of increased proficiency in reading should be in two different areas of study presented earlier in this section: English language, and study skills.

In the area of English language study, reading development is emphasized as a receptive language-art. In this regard, the student reacts to the written word received through reading, reconstructs verbal meanings through comprehension, and relates the ideas received to his background understandings as a basis for producing (composing) ideas in written language. Thus receiving and interpreting verbal meanings are recommended as the primary foci of reading improvement in English language study, for the reception of ideas through reading serves as an important source of verbal images for the production of written discourse.

On the other hand, the principal focus upon reading improvement in the study skills area is that of using reading as an indispensable tool in the execution of the multifaceted operations of college study. The students' increased competencies in the tool functions of reading, therefore, involve (1) the systematic upgrading of their skills in utilizing a repertory of reading rates suitable to the type of text; (2) the development of regular habits of establishing specific purposes for reading assignments to serve as tacit motivation for reading; (3) learning to use a study-reading formula, such as SQ3R, to maximize information-processing while reading and minimizing time and effort; (4) improving skills in assessing various types of written discourse through utilizing such different critical reading strategies as (a) identifying the author's intent and/or bias, (b) discriminating between opinions and facts, and

(c) isolating the main theses and their subordinate details in a reading assignment and being able to summarize, generalize, and categorize them; and (5) utilizing a variety of appropriate reference materials to satisfy designated assignment needs.

The pivotal role of reading in the attainment of a college education surely justifies the inclusion of reading improvement studies in all appropriate areas in the instructional system for high-risk students.

THE *WHAT* PARADIGM: CONCLUSION

The learning objectives and course content presented in the *what* of this instructional paradigm for high-risk students encompass the universally recognized basic tools-of-learning skills in mathematics and English language study, and the learning-to-learn competencies that undergird students' psychosocial adaptation to higher education. Not only does this paradigm endorse a sharply focused concentration upon these learning activities during the threshold program of studies, but also recommends continuing academic support in the functional application of these indispensable tools-of-learning in college mainstream studies for as long as students need them during their undergraduate career.

The cognitive and affective learning skills herein proposed will serve as synergetic vehicles to contribute to the realization of the purposes of this instructional system—the extension of equality of educational opportunity to all students admitted to American higher education.

The How: *Instructional Strategies—Andragogy vs Pedagogy, Organizational Patterns, Methods and Techniques, Staff Attributes*

In an extended metaphor, K. Patricia Cross (1979) makes a graphic comparison between American postsecondary education today and a typical superhighway. She draws an analogy between the problems resulting in each domain because of vastly increased, heterogeneous traffic within the past two decades. Superhighways today are beset with cars, trucks, and vans of every conceivable design, purpose, and potential; while American postsecondary education is besieged presently by students who possess the fullest dimensions of academic, demographic, and motivational heterogeneity.

Coping with the increased diversity of the traffic in both domains has required imaginative, productive problem solving. And even as American highways have developed engineering structures that have largely met the needs for change, so have promising new directions in teaching and learning evolved to some extent to meet the new demands in American higher education.

Despite the fact that reluctant and dilatory acceptance of the need for adapting to the exigencies of the student enrollment explosion has been the rule rather than the exception in all too many American colleges and universities, a growing body of knowledge about how students learn has emerged within the past ten to fifteen years. Additionally, the findings from psychological and pedagogical research about effective college teaching have expanded the information bank about instructional systems in higher education.

For the most part, three main sources of research have produced the most seminal findings concerning effective teaching-learning processes in higher education in response to post-1960s student enrollments—the Center for Research on Learning and Teaching (CRLT, the University of Michigan), The Fund for the Improvement of Postsecondary Education (FIPSE, USOE), and *CHANGE: The Magazine for Learning* (Reports on Teaching: Notable Improvements in American Undergraduate Teaching). A distillation of the literature from these three sources synthesized with empirical research about extant, exemplary programs for high-risk students, combined with the writer's relevant professional experiences are the bases of the *how* in this instructional paradigm.

The hallmarks of effective instruction for high-risk college students which follow will focus upon these synergetically related concerns: (1) the essential philosophical and psychological differences between *andragogy* and *pedagogy*, and the reasons why the former is superior to the latter in teaching high-risk students; (2) the organizational structures in the instructional delivery-system; (3) principles, methods, and techniques in high-risk instruction; and (4) attributes of prototype instructors and support staff.

ANDRAGOGY VS. PEDAGOGY

Today in America, the human developmental stages of childhood and adolescence are more attenuated and prolonged than in any other nation. Defining the attainment of adulthood, therefore, in our country is difficult because the concept is inextricably related to and influenced by economic, sociological, and psychological factors. Be that as it may, by using any of several generally accepted perceptions of adulthood, there are many more adults than before among the post-1960 student enrollees in American higher education. And these new-type college students possess an experiential maturity that endows them with "streetwiseness" and field-tested value systems from which vantage point they perceive of themselves as adult, and wish to be treated as such.

In earlier sections of this monograph the unreadiness of many college faculties to accept and to instruct effectively nontraditional students has been discussed. To a large extent, faculties have not been able to understand the maturity of these new-type students and their subcultural milieu. In this regard, the majority of college instructors have conducted instructional strategies which are deemed by nontraditional students to be personally demeaning and intellectually stultifying. It is the view of these students that they are often treated as though they were children. And indeed, many college faculties have been guilty of practicing *pedagogy* rather than *andragogy*.

The term *andragogy* has been used extensively in Scandinavian educational circles since the latter part of the nineteenth century to refer to the science of adult instruction (Knowles, 1970). In America, McClusky (1958), Kidd (1959), Jones (1959), and Knox (1977), among others, have been in the vanguard of educators who have initiated a "differential psychology of adults." They recognized the etymological misapplication of the term, pedagogy, to the teaching of adults and pioneered in the use of andragogy in reference to the education of postadolescents.

In this paradigm instructional strategies for high-risk college students must be soundly predicated upon an understanding of the basic premises of andragogy. Research into adults as learners has revealed significant differences between childhood and adult orientations to learning:

1. *Heterogeneity*. Adults as a group represent the full dimensions of human diversity—physically, cognitively, affectively, experientially, and idiosyncratically. On the other hand, children and youth living under the constraints of abbreviated time simply have not had the time to log that much of life and have more common, primitive bases of *realia*-to-be-experienced or learned. The things that adults need to learn or want to learn are so widely various that

the traditional pattern of group instruction focused upon undiagnosed status is counterproductive. Instructors of adults should be cognizant of the fact that, in any instructional episode, multiple variables related to the students' heterogeneity of aspiration, motivation, interest, and knowledge are impacting on the learning objectives and purposes.

2. *Autonomy*. Adults are voluntary participants in the learning situation while children and youth for the most part are not. The freedom of choice, independence of selection, and self-direction exercised by adult learners *ipso facto* totally conditions and qualifies all aspects of the teaching-learning syndrome. The teacher of adults who forgets that the students are *not* members of a passive, compliant, captive audience will build an irreparable barrier to and insurmountable rejection of the instructional interplay. The element of voluntary participation in education implies the need for alternatives to sole reliance on authoritarian, prescribed didacticism.

3. *Residuarity*. The adult learner is a veritable storehouse of codified information and structured knowledge. Unlike the child or youth, the adult's principal learning tasks seldom involve the encountering of totally new facts, information, or skills. Thus, the adult learner approaches most educational episodes with a broad background of meaningful (and partially understood and assimilated) perceptions, conceptualalizations, and generalizations. He is ready, therefore, to engage in integrational activities with any unfamiliar ideas by using techniques of comparison, abstraction, categorization, and functional subordination. By being aware of the residuary nature of the adult learner, the teacher wisely establishes a partnership in the learning process and focuses upon evoking, eliciting, and augmenting the student's background knowledge with as much concern as he devotes to the processing of new information and skills.

4. *Maturity*. Not all adult learners possess maturity, but the majority of them who do are aware of the uniqueness of their humanity, make their own decisions, and wish to be responsible for their own mistakes. The requirements and demands of the mature adult's present situation as well as his aspiring goals in life conjoin to dominate his learning commitments and predilections. Whereas in childhood and youth it is possible to impose and direct the learner in the attainment of exogenous objectives; in adult maturity, learning is most productive when the student is assisted in clarifying his own endogenous purposes. Having defined personal goals, the mature

adult is then ready to be counseled about realistic alternatives and strategies he may pursue in their attainment.

DELIVERY SYSTEMS: COURSES, LABORATORIES, COUNSELING, TUTORIALS, MAINSTREAM ACADEMIC SUPPORT, *AD HOC* WORKSHOPS

The instructional delivery-systems presented in this paradigm for high-risk college students are variegated, and they reflect an overriding educational commitment to serving individual and group pluralistic needs effectively. The quantity and quality of the courses, laboratories, and other aspects of the delivery-systems herein presented relate directly to findings about students' personal and academic status which are secured from diagnostic and needs-assessment processes. And it was established in earlier sections of this monograph that post-1960, nontraditional college students differ markedly from those in previous times in both academic proficiency and personal characteristics.

It should be indicated at the outset that students whose diagnostic instruments reveal seriously impeding deficits in the basic skills and the learning-to-learn competencies will require substantive adjustments in their initial curricula. Those who must enroll in a full threshold program—i.e., basic skills (in English and mathematics) and the learning-to-learn skills (orientation to higher education, study skills, personal development), should have limited access to mainstream, freshman courses. They should be permitted to take only the minimal, full-time student course load—customarily only two of the less demanding mainstream courses in conjunction with a complete "threshold" program. By reducing high-risk students' academic burdens in the first semesters of college study has been shown to heighten their chances for survival (Hawkins, 1978).

Cronbach (1967) and other researchers on teaching effectiveness have urged the investigation of learning variables other than rate of learning (which has received the lion's share of attention for several decades). Cronbach believed that the problem of individual differences is more complicated than dividing people into "fast" and "slow" learners. In fact, it takes no special knowledge of research to recognize that all people have unique, characteristic "styles" for collecting and organizing information into useful knowledge (Cross, 1977). In brief, people have specialized ways of using their minds, and these mental characteristics are now labeled *cognitive styles*, which have fundamental and pervasive importance to education. (Witkin, 1973)

Inasmuch as some students learn most effectively in interaction with others, while others learn best in solitary study, the delivery systems soon to be proposed in this paradigm are many and varied as to locus, size, and management. The case in point is that learning environments and scenarios that present multiple approaches are likely to approximate and accommodate to the variability in students' learning styles. The instructional modalities that follow have field-tested effectiveness for high-risk students:

1. *classroom-based, small-group (circa 15 students), teacher-directed instruction*—for students who respond to didactic profferings;
2. *classroom-based, small-group (circa 15 students), teacher/student partnership-learning*—for students who are mature enough to engage in contract-learning in an evocative climate (i.e., students who can assume responsibility for binding themselves to learning objectives in light of their diagnosed academic deficits);
3. *classroom-based, teacher-supervised, mastery-learning*—for students who prosper with variable time-frames in self-pacing modules assisted by intermittent teacher assistance;
4. *laboratory-based, quasi-independent, mastery-learning, self-paced-learning systems*, e.g., personalized system of instruction (PSI); audio-tutorial(AT); or computer-assisted instruction (CAI)—for students who can progress in a relatively self-managed manner through receiving immediate feedback as to the correctness of their responses in basic skills studies;
5. *peer tutorials in basic skills studies*—for students who respond to one-to-one instruction by their peers with less hostility or fear than they do to teachers;
6. *peer tutorials in mainstream courses*—for students who need one-to-one, on-going assistance in general information, clarifying expatiation, and the synthesizing of ideas;
7. ad hoc, *small-group, basic skills workshops*—for students who have similar or identical topical problems of especial seriousness that can be resolved in short-term, targeted attention in directed sessions that are parallel and supportive to the regular course;
8. *clinical services*—*ad hoc*, emergency, and ongoing assistance for students who encounter unforeseen or undiagnosed academic and/or adjustment problems;
9. *counseling*—for all students, regardless of their academic status,

in order that they may receive assistance in sharpening their personal identification, assess their idiosyncratic nature, become oriented to higher education, and set academic, personal, and vocational goals;

10. *"dial-for-help"*—for students who encounter urgent learning problems (without benefit of their customary learning aids) that can be resolved by just a word or short explanation (e.g., Is it necessary to use a dieresis over the second *o* in cooperation?"), a resource reference, or a reinforcing colloquy.

11. *campus radio/tv targeted-academic reinforcement services*—for students who respond to information and skills that are dispensed in modern, mass-media packages; and if they sense this program is collaboratively operated by students and the learning assistance program, it has the additional benefit of having peer support.

In *Beyond the Open Door*, Cross (1971) proposed a "pluralistic model" for coping with the academic and personal diversity of post-1960s, nontraditional college enrollees. Cross championed as the primary task of higher education today a broadening of the objectives and focus of a college education beyond the narrow concern with the development of excellence in information processing. Adequate skills in working with things and people are needed in this era, also, and their development cannot be left to extracurricular activities and chance. They must be developed concurrently and concomitantly in the college program of studies in diverse interpersonal contexts along with developing skill in the manipulation of ideas. The teaching-learning activities focused upon in the various delivery-systems may be basically remedial, compensatory, or developmental in nature; nonetheless, they all conceptually contribute to the umbrella model, pluralistic, and may be subsumed under it.

The preceding instructional delivery-systems provide a variety of educational settings, multimedia resources, and dissimilar managements in which multimodal teaching-learning scenarios may transpire. Differences in class sizes, settings, authority, objectives, tenure and the like are designed to match or approximate student differences in cognitive style and learning predilections. Whereas, for example, some students respond most potently to intellectual stimulation received from their peers, others progress most effectively in small groups in relatively teacher-dominated classrooms; and still other students function with greatest ease in laboratory settings in which they are primarily self-directed in the learning activities. By increasing student choices and alternative educational strategies, it is highly probable that we have increased the delivery of productive learning experiences.

PRINCIPLES, METHODS, AND TECHNIQUES IN HIGH-RISK INSTRUCTION

For several decades prior to the recent college enrollment boom of vastly heterogeneous students, elementary and secondary levels of American public education had become firmly committed to philosophical assumptions concerning human differences. Empirical evidence about student intravariability and individual differences within the context of the school's demands for normative behavior had led to the espousal of holistic theories of human development by Gesell (1940), Havighurst (1953), and Prescott (1957). These distinguished human-development psychologists, along with others, stressed the indivisibility and uniqueness of the individual and the inherent interrelatedness of a human's physical, social, affective, and cognitive development. The implications from their research and theories have had far-reaching affects on American pedagogy. The paramount principle applied from human-development research is that the educative process must embody a recognition of the pluralistic nature of each individual's capacities, and must develop his constellation of abilities.

Increasingly since the late 1960s, as American college enrollments have virtually approximated the maximum diversity of students on the elementary and secondary levels, a gradual incorporation of the basic principles and assumptions about human individuality are to be found in exemplary higher education instructional systems. These principles and assumptions are an amalgam of ethical, religious, philosophical, sociological, and psychological premises; and many of them have been subjected vigorously to scientific investigation. Some widely accepted principles and assumptions follow, and upon them rest those precollege and postsecondary instructional programs deemed to be most productive with academically and personally diverse students.

1. Each individual is different from every other one and should have the right to strive for his or her optimum, unique development.
2. Each human being is valuable (of worth, importance, significance, merit) and should be treated at all times in ways that do not abridge rights and that permit him or her to function with dignity and self-respect.

3. Human behavior is caused and is meaningful, and the causes that underlie behavior as well as the meanings thereof are both many and varied.

4. Each human being is an indivisible, dynamic energy system consisting of interlocking, interrelated, interdependent physical, social, affective, and cognitive systems. The emergence of each distinctive human personality is the by-product of the mutual interplay of the foregoing systems in response to environmental forces.

5. Conceptualizations of learning potential as being genetically predetermined and fixed, and the nature of learning as being a mechanistic, linear, additive process are no longer tenable in light of recent research. Learning potential is conceived today as being creatable through continuous transactions between the organism and the environment and is modifiable in both rate and sequence. And today the nature of learning is perceived as being a holistic response and unfolding of the individual to a *Gestalten*-type environment in continuous self-renewing, self-organizing transactions.

The views of human individuality and transactional learning expressed in the foregoing passage undergird and permeate the instructional principles, methods, techniques, and related strategies which this paradigm endorses. The multidimensional teaching-learning practices that follow reflect the andragogical philosophy presented in an earlier section, and they mirror a conscious departure from traditional, monodimensional college instruction.

Planned/Purposeful/Focused

A commitment to educational pluralism within the context of the advocacy of equality of educational opportunity in a program for high-risk college students implies as well a dedication to education for *each* as well as education for *all*. Only through prolific, continuous, scrupulous planning on several levels is it possible to render the multiple, variegated services to the students that the practice of educational pluralism encompasses.

Planning is the nucleus of the very matrix of an effective learning assistance program, and it is the position in this paradigm that planning must be inextricably interwoven into all aspects of the program's *modus operandi*. In preplanning activities, in which the program is designed, decisions are made concerning such issues as the program's administrative locus and hierarchy, philosophical orientation, the dimensions of the program, admissions criteria, curriculum foci, instructional objectives, budget and financial support, physical resources and equipment, and staffing needs and selection criteria.

After the establishment of a learning assistance program, the planning of ongoing arrangements is necessary that encompasses such matters as class scheduling, entry-level and exit-level course criteria, monitoring and evaluation procedures, recordkeeping, campus outreach and tangential services, staff development, and (most importantly) specific classroom and laboratory instructional practices.

Diagnostic/Prescriptive

Establishing students' entry levels in all components of study through the administration of various, appropriate standardized, intramural, and modular tests is the essential, preliminary procedure. (The more reference groups to whom students are compared, the more descriptive and informative are the test findings.) Preinstructional diagnosis (a) eliminates wasteful course redundancy, (b) provides a valid basis for content selection, (c) supplies vital information for developing individual student prescriptions for study, and (d) gives students accurate data about their skills mastery and competencies which can serve as personal base levels for directed study and independent laboratory work.

Diagnosing readiness or status for learning is virtually a *sine qua non* procedure in learning assistance programs which largely utilize mastery learning and self-paced learning systems. And inasmuch as self-paced learning modules are making a significant impact on mainstream university teaching in the natural sciences (especially in biology, physics, and engineering), regular diagnostic procedures have become increasingly an accepted part of effective college teaching (Cross, 1977).

The interdependent relationship between mastery learning and diagnostic testing resides in the fact that a learner must attain a high level of competence in a given unit or module before he may progress to the next, higher unit in the sequence of study. The immediate confirmation of successful or failing performance received from a modular test (i.e., formative evaluation) gives the student a type of feedback which is self-generating. Feedback on progress provides explicit guidance to the student—not normative grading, and with appropriate "correctives" (prescriptive assignments) available, students can profit from their errors.

Diagnostic findings, in addition to the aforementioned uses, are synergetically related to the materials of instruction to be suggested for a particular learner, to the selection of indicated methods of instruction, and to the type of evaluations which will be utilized to assess student progress. Ascertaining the present status of students prior to organizing and executing instructional strategies influences and facilitates all aspects of the teaching-learning interplay.

Individualized/Personalized

Understanding and accepting the inimitable uniqueness of human beings should lead *ipso facto* to the educational practice of *individualizing and personalizing instruction*. The term *individualizing* must not be confused with individual instruction. (The latter should be used in reference to one-to-one tutoring.) The basic principles that follow are widely accepted in educational circles on all levels as essential factors in individualized/personalized instruction, and they pay rich dividends when utilized in learning assistance programs for high-risk students:

1. Students are active rather than passive participants in the teaching-learning interplays. The teacher is a manager and facilitator in the learning environment—he or she prepares materials, diagnoses status, prescribes, motivates, and serves as a resource. Student "doing" rather than teacher "telling" is the rule as didacticism is sidelined in favor of heurism.

2. Students are provided continuous, explicit information about their academic status. Not only do entry-level assessments supply precourse information to the students about their specific strengths and weaknesses in each subject, but also ongoing modular and unit tests give systematic feedback on student progress. Prescriptions for resolving deficits and for attaining the course objectives are collaboratively developed by students and teachers in light of initial and ongoing diagnosis.

3. In recognition of individual differences in rate of learning, mastery and self-pacing learning are featured (especially in basic skills courses). Various types of hard- and software programmed

instruction are used, as well as computer-assisted programs and materials.

4. In classroom instructional settings when small groups of students have a common information need, the teacher uses multidimensional topical presentations. Every effort is made to compensate for differences in comprehension and perception by giving several examples and illustrations of a skill or concept and by using many synonymous and analogous terms. Students are encouraged consistently to draw upon their own bountiful, unique, personal experiences to augment and enrich explanations, illustrations, and perspectives on the topic under study.

5. In recognition of student differences in cognitive and learning styles, individualized/personalized instruction provides students (1) systematic understanding of their distinctive cognitive styles, and (2) alternative instructional procedures and materials in order to accommodate these differences.

In this paradigm it is suggested that in the learning-to-learn program of studies a systematic analysis of each student's learning predilections be mapped. A profile of students' distinctive approaches in information processing can be developed from a series of tests for this purpose, such as the one by Hill (1971). From the data revealed in such instruments, students are able to discover, for example, whether they are field-independent or field-dependent, i.e., whether they have an analytical or a global way of perceiving information or situations. They are able to find out, also, such things as the intensity or extensiveness of their attention deployment; their breadth of categorizing; their consistency or inconsistency in narrowly or broadly conceptualizing; and their reflectiveness or impulsivity in developing hypotheses when processing information.

Faculty awareness of student variability in cognition should result in conscious attempts to assist students in diversifying their learning strategies through dissimilar learning situations and approaches. For this reason, this paradigm endorses the following examples of varied learning settings and tasks: (1) opportunities for learning in group interaction, as well as periods for lone study and contemplation; (2) opportunities for watching, listening, and reading, as well as times for speaking, directing, and personally demonstrating; (3) opportunities to receive planned, systematic, didactic, methodical guidance, and times for informal, heuristic, exploratory study; and (4) opportunities to engage in intuitive, global, divergent learning tasks, and times for participating in empirical, restricted, convergent tasks.

Earlier sections of this monograph made the point that historically American higher education has been indifferent to the quality of teaching-learning interplays within the classroom. The prevalent lack of interest in pedagogy is unquestionably superseded as well by any knowledge of or interest in andragogy—the instructional methods herein recommended for teaching adults. At this point a strong case is made for the desirability of learning assistance instructors (and for that matter, college teachers in general) to develop and utilize a repetory of planned, systematic, teaching-learning strategies. The guides that follow are recommended approaches in a teacher-directed learning episode:

1. In a brief introduction to the lesson, the teacher assists the students in "setting-the-stage" for the day's class through reviewing briefly the primary focus of the preceding lesson. Using the course syllabus, the topic, concept, or skill for the class session is established, and its relevance to past learnings is clarified. Some attention is given, also, to the general place of today's topic in the overall purpose of the course.

This initial step in a developmental lesson serves as the orientation. It allows students to become slightly familiar with the material to be learned, and to establish linkages with significant information with which they are already comfortable. The feeling that the topic is perhaps a little of old wine in new bottles increases the students' idiosyncratic readiness for and receptivity to the entire learning episode.

2. In the next phase of the lesson, the topic or skill to be learned is presented in sharply focused, clear, unambiguous terms. In an effort to augment and enhance student understanding of the newly introduced materials, the teacher uses a multiplicity of examples, illustrations, and synonymous terms to broaden the students' repertory of references. The students are encouraged to participate actively in this "in-other-words" game, and to suggest additional, clarifying examples from their experiential backgrounds. (Misconceptions frequently surface at this point, and meaningful, redundant expatiation can transpire.)

Although the subject-under-study may be initially presented by the teacher in a traditional lecture (and some concepts are best served in this manner), it is strongly recommended in this paradigm that other ways of effecting the class presentation be tried. For example, a specifically assigned student or team of students occasionally may serve as presenters. Audiovisual equipment, programmed guides, directed reading of supplementary texts, and instructional games may all be used productively.

This step may be characterized as the nucleus of the lesson, for the presentation of previously unlearned material is surely the kernel around which both student and course growth and development transpire. It cannot be overemphasized that the greater the number of meaningful expatiations about the new material contributed by students and teacher, and the greater the number of relevant examples given, the greater the chances are that students will set up meaningful linkages between the new material and ideas previously learned. And the greater the number of linkages, the greater are the chances for retrieving and utilizing knowledge.

3. Developmental lessons terminate with increased effectiveness when explicitly planned *synthesizing* and *summarizing* activities reinforce the preceding instructional interactions. During this final step in the lesson, students are encouraged to raise questions about unclear concepts, to synthesize the new information into previously learned materials, compare and contrast the new information with former conceptualizations, and to speculate about the possible relationship of the current topic to the entire course content.

Out-of-class assignments along with laboratory, self-pacing study serve as natural extensions of directed classroom learning. Assignments that have been thoughtfully planned are especially fruitful media through which to personalize and individualize developmental courses. By directing students to multiple, relevant resources in quest of additional information, the perspectives on any topic under study will be sharply broadened and deepened. And at the same time, students' unique interests and predilections will be tapped and stimulated. The cyclic benefits to the course will be realized when the sharing of diverse research and perspectives by the students can become the transitional preview and orientation for the succeeding topic in the course.

STAFF ATTRIBUTES: MENTORING, INSTRUCTING, TUTELAGE

There are contrasting opinions in educational circles about the most propitious environment for fostering effective teaching and learning. There is an equal lack of unanimity about the characteristics that teachers should have in order to guide productive learning. Essentially these disagreements reside in debates between behaviorists and humanists concerning the most promising approaches to education. On the one hand behaviorists stress the application of product-oriented scientific principles; while on the other, humanists emphasize the need for idiosyncratic attention and human warmth (Markle, 1970). Behaviorists and humanists both agree, nonetheless, that the effective teacher is the dynamic fulcrum in the teaching-learning syndrome.

Throughout the history of education, several images or models have emerged of the ideal teacher and the effective teaching environment. These images blend elements from behavioristic and humanistic learning theory and may be identified in unequal proportions in former and contemporary educational settings. Thelen (1954) categorized some of the more antiquated teaching-learning situations in the following metaphoric terms: the "Socratic discussion," the "boss-employee," the "good old team," the "business deal," the "guided tour," the "town meeting," the "army model," and "the apprenticeship."

The foregoing models are basically oriented toward behavioristic, authoritarian principles; and although they may be identified to some extent in contemporary settings on all levels of education, five newer models have emerged which have humanistic attributes which naturally yield individualized/personalized practices. These reform models have been discussed in chapter one of this monograph; thus only their titles with brief identification will be presented at this point: the *bazaar* model (freedom of choice); the *amusement park* (directed enticement of learners to an array of choices); the *praxis* model (uniting theory, practice, knowledge, and first-hand action); the *"just-be"* model (living and experiencing as education); and the *Siddhartha* model (education as a personal quest in self-actualization).

The point has been belabored throughout this monograph that a mutually supportive, synergetic relationship must exist between all facets of an instructional system. The staff characteristics to be subscribed to in this section, therefore, are desirable or undesirable only in terms of the philosophy and purposes of the staff's learning assistance program. In a learning assistance program staff composed of teachers, counselors, laboratory specialists (audiovisual equipment specialists), and student tutors, some attributes may be identified that should be common to all of these workers; while some traits and skills are related to their service role. Calling upon past and present perceptions of effective environments for learning, and relating these perceptions to the philosophical framework and the explicit *what* and *how* in this paradigm, it is possible to delineate both general and special attributes of the staff.

The *general attributes* all learning assistance program staff should possess are skills in *interpersonal relations*. It is the position in this paradigm that these skills are best classified as *mentoring* skills—a term explicated with exceptional insight by the United States Department of Labor in its *Dictionary of Occupational Titles* (DOT). *Mentoring* involves "dealing with individuals in terms of their total personality in order to advise, counsel, and/or guide them." At the heart of mentoring is the mentor's sensitivity to the uniqueness, worthiness, and efficacy of each human being. This sensitivity enhances the responsiveness and reactivity of the mentor in positive ways to the multiple needs of others. The phrases that follow are the nuclei of mentoring behaviors devised by Breen (1975) as modifications of the DOT list, and are herein proposed for the interpersonal repertory of the staff of a learning assistance program with some minor changes:

. . . listens with genuine concern
. . . asks appropriate questions
. . . reflects back feeling and informational responses
. . . guides conversation
. . . diagnoses and evaluates feelings and information
. . . feeds back diagnoses
. . . makes suggestions
. . . evokes suggestions for possible problem solving
. . . presents necessary information, explains, gives examples
. . . forecasts possible outcomes, predicts consequences
. . . reviews alternative courses of action
. . . gives assurances and support
. . . reinforces positive actions as motivational forces
. . . provides feedback and evaluation of progress
. . . promotes the free flow of two-way communication
. . . reflects accepted standards, purposes, and program goals
. . . reconciles opposing viewpoints
. . . assists in the collaborative amelioration of problems
. . . encourages self-definition
. . . radiates sincere concern and positive regard
. . . concentrates on the building of strengths
. . . coaxes individuals to elaborate on thoughts and feelings
. . . radiates interest and enthusiasm

The foregoing interpersonal skills may be thought of as the "helping skills," and Carkhuff (1969) and others have suggested that all workers in the social services should be skillful in the dimensions of successful helping. It is the position in this paradigm that the mentoring skills are basically humanistic helping skills, and that empathetic understanding is the *sine qua non* of the general attributes required of all learning assistance staff.

The special, *task-related, product-oriented services* of learning assistance teachers, counselors, laboratory A/V specialists, and student-tutors require designated academic credentials and competencies in English, mathematics, study skills, personal and career counseling, and audiovisual equipment and materials. It is the position in this paradigm that appropriate screening procedures be instituted to guarantee the employment of staff who have functional competence in all of the above positions. In addition to academic credentials and the demonstrated proof thereof, the attributes that follow are herein endorsed for the staff which relate to the execution of their designated tutelary roles:

1. In their roles as guiders of student development in the skills of turning information into knowledge, learning assistance staff should possess *cognitive flexibility*. In light of wide differences in student learning styles and experiential backgrounds, it is mandatory that in directed-learning situations the staff is able to extend and clarify meanings by shifting from the familiar and known to the unfamiliar and obscure. This is accomplished most effectively in a multiplicity of verbal interplays in which the metaphor and analogy are used frequently and precisely.

2. In all of their tutelary roles, the staff should maintain a *humanistic learning environment* in which students feel free to falter (as well as discover techniques for succeeding) without the fear of rejection in a climate of unconditional regard.

3. The staff should be capable of utilizing *a repertory of instructional modes, styles, skills, methods, and techniques*. (The old saying, "there is more than one way to skin a cat," is recognized as a regular strategy in teaching-learning interplays.) The overriding thrust of the instruction, counseling, and tutoring should be the development of students' abilities to secure broad meanings and understandings through interpreting and synthesizing information, rather than accumulating isolated, fragmented facts through rote memory.

4. Inasmuch as effective learning is best promoted when diagnostic measures, instructional objectives, learning aids, teaching strategies, and evaluative procedures are mutually and collaboratively supportive, the staff should understand and utilize *synergetic principles*.

Inasmuch as the learning assistance staff play pivotal roles in the functioning of the totality of the program, it is critical that the staff possess impressive mentoring and tutelary skills and attributes. The constellation of interpersonal skills and tutelary attributes presented in the foregoing section should equip the staff for making significant contributions to the ultimate success of the program.

THE *HOW* PARADIGM: Conclusion

The proposals presented in the foregoing sections about productive instructional practices for high-risk students are, in essence, a metaphorical "instructional zygote." This zygote embodies the "marriage" of behavioristic, product-oriented, basic skills improvement to humanistic, person-oriented, idiosyncratic development in a "pluralistic" model. And this marriage of the information and skills-processing areas of higher education to the human development concerns constitutes the most challenging instructional problem currently facing colleges and universities. Not only is this so in learning assistance programs, but also in the mainstream college curricula.

It was suggested in the *how* discussions that accepting the adult status of college students could lead to the effective practice of andragogy. Then, too, by utilizing a multiplicity of instructional delivery systems, it was possible to approximate rewardingly the academic heterogeneity and cognitive styles of the students. The overriding importance of all types of instructional planning on various levels in learning assistance programs was emphasized, and the significance of consciously providing for human variability in all teaching-learning interactions was stressed. And finally, the marriage of mentoring and tutelary skills and attributes in faculty and staff was proposed for maximum student development.

The How Well: *Monitoring, Assessing, Evaluating*

Prior to the student unrest on American campuses in the 1960s when undergraduates expressed their disenchantment and dissatisfaction with college instructional practices, few institutions of higher education engaged in the evaluation of instructional programs with any degree of purposefulness or regularity. Only when accrediting agencies made their periodic reviews of the overall status of a college or university were academic programs (with few exceptions) submitted to explicit scrutiny. (Brubacher and Rudy, 1976)

Concurrent with campus unrest in the 1960s came the multifaceted problems associated with the enrollment boom of underprepared students for higher education. In earlier sections of this monograph the point was made that these two unexpected forces challenged the very foundations of traditional higher education in America. The need for sensitive, effective, productive undergraduate teaching and learning became apparent to all.

Unlike traditional, mainstream curricula and programs of study, learning assistance programs from the outset were expected to prove their worth through systematic evaluation. Perhaps because skills programs are viewed as being peripheral to the established mission of a college, and because their high-risk clients were begrudgingly accepted on many campuses, basic skills programs were requested to demonstrate their effectiveness in aiding students. (See Maxwell, 1979, chapter six)

Grant and Hoeber (1978) among others have noted the generally undistinguished quality of the initial evaluative studies which were made of learning assistance programs and attribute their weakness to hastily, poorly designed, visionary program goals. Identifying clearly defined, measurable goals for a learning assistance program is admittedly not easy, however. As has been discussed in another section of this monograph, the bottom-line question is: How much improvement realistically and feasibly can be expected in a one- or two-semester program to make up for twelve years of unsuccessful education? Surely a learning assistance program must face that question forthrightly and provide both threshold and ongoing support programs for high-risk students, as this paradigm has proposed.

What should be the focus of learning assistance program evaluation? For what convincing reason is the worth, validity, or productivity of the program being assessed? In many instances, learning assistance programs have evaluated cost-effectiveness in response to a growing concern about educational accountability from state, federal, and private funding agencies (Carman, 1971; Garms, 1971). In other instances the evaluative research has focused upon subjective, judgmental, phenomenological viewpoints and reactions of both students and staff (Ball, 1975); and in still other programs the effectiveness of instructional methodology and the relevance of the curriculum content have been measured. Regardless of the focus, it is generally agreed today that there must be a positive, synergetic relationship between the purpose of the evaluation and the established purposes of the total program.

Over the past ten years as learning assistance programs have become the rule rather than the exception in American institutions of higher education, substantive guides have developed from an increasing consensus about the most fruitful ways to evaluate these programs. Of particular merit in this regard is the *Final Report of National Project II, Alternatives to the Revolving Door* (Ball, n.d.), in which emerging differences are delineated between learning assistance program evaluation and traditional, "pure," "abstract" research. Learning assistance program evaluation is seen as being essentially *decision-oriented* (i.e., primarily concerned with providing timely, relevant, comprehensible feedback [information] for use in pragmatic, current, operational activities). On the other hand, basic research is defined as being primarily new *knowledge-oriented* (i.e., concerned with the discovery of new information through rigorous, controlled, scientific methods).

In light of the overriding commitment in this instructional paradigm to a pluralistic model of education that embraces a philosophy of education for *each* as well as education for *all* (i.e., not only equality of educational opportunity for diverse student populations, but also quality of education within the students' diagnosed needs and career aspirations), the evaluative research proposed in this paradigm is twofold:

> *First*, there should be monitoring, assessing, and evaluating procedures that document why, where, when, and how the purposes of the program are attained; and
>
> *Second*, there should be monitoring, assessing, and evaluating processes that document the effects and affects of the accomplished purposes of the program.

The questions that follow are illustrative of the concerns in the first areas of evaluation: (1) What academic factors relate to students' success in the learning assistance program? (SAT scores? A designated instructional strategy? Modular test scores? Program diagnostic test scores? High school grade-point average? A designated audiovisual medium? Tenure in the program? CEEB Achievement Test scores? etc.); and (2) What nonacademic factors relate to students' success in the learning assistance program? (Sex of the student? Age? Attendance? Career aspirations? Self-concepts and motivation? Socioeconomic status? Financial aid? etc.)

The criteria that follow are illustrative of the foci in the second area of evaluation: percentages of enrollees who receive the baccalaureate degrees in stated numbers of semesters; growth scores on standardized tests of achievement; grade-point averages of enrollees in mainstream college courses; student reactions to teacher and course effectiveness; effects of the program's English course on student success in mainstream English studies; faculty and staff attitudes toward the program; effects of the program's mathematics course on student success in mainstream mathematics studies; impact of the program on the campus as a whole; effects of study skills course on success in mainstream courses; attrition rate of learning assistance program enrollees compared to mainstream students; etc.

THE *HOW WELL* PARADIGM: Conclusion

Conducting appropriate evaluation in order to determine how well a learning assistance program is functioning is a critically necessary, justifiable program operation. Some of the evaluative research strategies proposed in the foregoing section are *formative* in nature while others are *summative*, and both types are herein recommended as essential to balanced program effectiveness. On the one hand, it is important to receive timely feedback about the strengths or weaknesses of various ongoing operations in order to conduct indicated program modifications. On the other hand, assessing the status of the attainment of intended and/or unintended outcomes have a contribution to make, also, to the productivity or ineffectiveness of a program.

The evaluative research procedures proposed in this paradigm, it must be reiterated, should include continually the monitoring and assessing through explicitly focused strategems the learning assistance program's progress in realizing its commitment to equality and quality of education.

Summary

Chapter four contains the nucleus of this monograph. The *why*, *what*, *how*, and *how well* of an instructional system for high-risk college students were presented successively and are, in essence, an amalgam of theoretical perspectives, empirical data, and the author's experiential impressions concerning productive teaching and learning practices for today's nontraditional students. The synthesizing element in the chapter was the concept of educational pluralism, because under this concept a full panoply of instructional strategies may be accommodated.

The *why* section focused upon the central purpose of equality and quality of educational opportunity; the *what* section presented the dual dimensions of product-oriented, basic-skills studies conjoined with human-oriented, personal-skills developmental areas; in the *how* section a multiplicity of instructional delivery-systems were explicated in the interest of suggesting ways to meet student differences in cognitive styles; and in the *how well* section a case was made for the regular inclusion of program monitoring, assessing, and evaluating.

In its entirety, chapter four is an attempt to make a contribution in answer to John Garner's query: "Can we be equal and excellent too?"

Chapter 5

TAKING STOCK—MEETING THE CHALLENGE

Introduction

At some point in some way in each of the preceding chapters, reference was made to the vast, fundamental impact on American higher education resulting from the more than triplication in student enrollment since the 1960s. In the opinion of many segments of the educational establishment, the ferment in American postsecondary education is the *de facto*, if not *de jure*, second, great revolution in our colleges and universities. And even as the first, great higher educational revolution—the land-grant college development in the late nineteenth century—profoundly influenced the basic perceptions and university practices in that era, so has (and shall) this sharp increase in accessibility transformed today's institutions.

The field of educational sociology has propagated unendingly its belief and dedication to the maxim—education must be resonant with the real world. Its equally renowned corollary is that as the nature of the world changes, so must societal institutions likewise change. It is possible to reinforce the foregoing maxim by referring in passing to Charles Darwin's ageless dictum—form follows function (purpose fathers structure). And within the context of the foci in this monograph, it may be stated that outmoded forms and practices in American higher education must change to conform to the new demands of the new purposes which today's reality makes.

The position of this monograph is that, in the United States, higher education can no longer afford the luxury of a protracted, convoluted dialogue pertaining to the indicated changes which present reality demands; rather, the very continuance of public support dictates addressing this problem with vigor, imagination, and immediacy. In both the Introduction and Preface of this monograph it was suggested that a case could be made for utilizing virtually all of the procedures and practices of high-risk instructional strategies with mainstream college students, also. In light of current knowledge about human variability, both within and between individuals, the broadening of pluralistic approaches in teaching and learning to all college education is reasonable. And providing multidimensional opportunities for the development of the full-range of students' traits and characteristics in addition to their monodimensional information-processing abilities, will be a realistic response to the needs of the kind of society in which we now find ourselves.

In this final chapter, stock will be taken through a backward look and assessment of the lessons learned in higher education from the "tumultous '60s" and the "unresolved '70s." Goals for the 1980s and 1990s will be projected by recommending feasible methods of transferring and applying high-risk student instructional practices to mainstream courses in the humanities, natural, and social sciences. Then, looking ahead to the twenty-first century, the chapter will conclude with recommended guides for effective college instruction that will meet the demands of the marketplace.

The Tumultous '60s

Prior to the early 1960s, only small numbers of American college students gave any indication that they had strong or abiding interests in or convictions about social and political issues and problems. In fact, unlike their European and Latin American counterparts, the American college student could be characterized frankly as being socially and politically immature, indifferent, and apathetic. Thus, with the advent of student activism in the early 1960s, American colleges and universities were as a group generally surprised, unprepared, and confounded in their initial attempts to understand, accept, and/or cope with the new genre of student. (See Brubacher and Rudy, 1976, *passim*, chapter sixteen.)

Analyses of American campus unrest in the 1960s have been many and varied. (See Jencks and Reisman, 1968; Horowitz and Friedland,

1970; Schwab, 1969; Roszak, 1969.) Some of the widely recognized and disseminated studies have attributed the unexpected, combustible, anomalous behavior at that time of sizeable numbers of college students to any one or a combination of the following factors: (1) the customary social ferment, dislocation, and acceleration resulting from war (World War II); (2) the advent of the "nuclear age" and all of its portents; (3) the civil rights movement with which college-age students could identify; (4) the renewal of the military draft for the "unjust" and undeclared Vietnam War; (5) disenchantment with and rejection of their parents' generation, which had justified the Vietnam War; (6) the communications revolution that had induced increased social and personal maturity in college-age students through depicting the full range of the human experience; and (7) a general restiveness and sense of disorientation caused by the accelerated change of the "future shock" nature of our era.

The preceding psycho-socio-political factors and concerns were translated into the following campus protest behaviors by the students of the 1960s: (1) demands for increased "student power" in such substantive college administrative decisions as faculty selection, promotion, tenure, and dismissal; (2) demands for increased "participatory democracy" in parietal arrangements; (3) unconditional requests for the extension of "student rights" to include the Constitutional guarantees of the First, Fifth, and Fourteenth Amendments—freedom of speech, the right of due process, and freedom of peaceable assembly; and (4) boisterous, aggressive, contemptuous, irrational rejection of any and all perceived aspects of collegiate paternalism. The parameters and dimensions of student behavior varied on all types of campuses in accordance with the degree of the commitment to nihilistic, anarchistic, or existentialistic dogma.

Eventually, student unrest and protest in the 1960s broadened its scope and focus to include the very heart of higher educational processes—the nature of the college curriculum content, and the quality of the instructional practices. And the legacies of these student activities left their identifiable imprint upon the overall workings of American higher education. Of special interest to this monograph is that no longer are policies and standards relating to faculty, instructional systems, and curriculum content the exclusive domain of American college administration and faculty. The rise of student power in the 1960s contributed irrevocably to a definition of accountability in American higher education. It is a definition that includes a continuing sensitivity to role and rights of students as the ultimate clients and consumers in the educative process.

The Unresolved '70s

In a retrospective article about the 1970s in the *Washington Post* (December 6, 1979) which Henry Allen entitled, "The Big '70s Burnout," he generally derided what he perceived in that decade as being a mammoth snafu of the lofty concerns and high promises of the activists of the 1960s. Allen pointed scathingly at the rise in cults, exotic religions, political corruption, the "laid back" philosophy, and "looking-out-for-#1" as all signs of a society which had become disoriented, effete, and sterile. He found the general preoccupation with self as evidence that the '70s decade, the "me generation," was spiritually and intellectually feckless.

Some of Allen's perceptions of the mood in the American society-at-large have been noted as well in the mood of students in higher education during the 1970s. In fact, some observers of the campus scene have called the 1970's decade the great "turnabout." When compared with their obstreperous, alienated 1960s' counterparts, the '70s students were civil and tractable. Accompanying the return to civility to campuses in the '70s was an identifiable return of previously rejected middle-class values as witnessed by a resurgence of student interest in academic accomplishment and career preparation.

There is perhaps some merit in examining briefly perceptions of the 180-degree turn in American student conduct during the 1970s. A concatenation of psychological, philosophical, sociological, and economic factors are involved in the explanations of the observable diminution in previously disruptve student behavior. There are some observers who argue that the lessening in activism was a natural, Hegelian, antithetical reaction to the stridently espoused thesis-of-dissent in the 1960s. Emotional fatigue, it is proposed, is an expected by-product of excessive, emotional behavior. There are other analysts of the '70s who attribute the "turnabout" to the ending of the Vietnam War and the military draft—in other words, those two endings preempted the *cause célèbres* of the student revolution and left them with no prime target to shout about. Then there are still other interpreters of the '70s who argue that the answer resides in the advent of post-Vietnam War economic dislocations due to inflation, which have radically changed in some measure many aspects of our national standard of living. All of the foregoing factors are perceived as being "tranquilizing" forces which generated student "inwardizing" behaviors. (See Brubacher and Rudy, 1976, *passim*, chapter sixteen.)

The abatement of student activism in the 1970s gave American higher education a much needed hiatus in which it could assimilate, consolidate, reintegrate, adjust, adapt, and plan to unify the by-products of the revolutionary 1960s. It must not be forgotten that the issues and problems facing American higher education in the 1970s were bifurcated—the legacies of student activism pertaining to changes in governance, curriculum, and instruction; and the enrollment boom which vastly increased academic heterogeneity. As American postsecondary institutions attempted to cope with these two challenges, ongoing dialectics transpired among and between their students, faculties, administrators, and governing boards about their schools' future role, mission, structure, and operation. In essence, American colleges and universities were called upon to modify in various ways long-established, conservative policies and practices in a relatively short period of time. They were expected to synthesize conventional, accepted ways of doing things and novel, untested procedures into a new *modus operandi*. Needless to say, the reconstructing and resolving activities in American postsecondary education during the 1970s were some of the most momentous and portentous tasks ever to be undertaken in its history. And our present understanding of the *Gestalten* involved alerts us to the fact that colleges and universities in their entirety have been affected in some measure, directly or indirectly, by the changes effected in any of their parts.

Rare indeed today is the American college or university that does not enter the 1980s with evidences of reconstructive accommodation to student demands for increased participatory democracy in governance and curriculum decisions. Equally exceptional is an institution which does not have some type of specialized instructional program to meet the needs of new entrants who enroll with vast academic diversity. In some instances the governance and curriculum adjustments and modifications have been merely superficial, Draconian-type attempts to force square pegs into traditional, round holes. In other instances, colleges and universities have begun thoughtfully to conceptualize and thoroughly develop comprehensive changes in their programs of study in response to the current requirements of today's student populations.

In the next section of this chapter, "Goals for the 1980s and 1990s: The Coming Age of College Instruction," selected guides from exemplary learning assistance programs will be fused with relevant sections of this monograph's chapter four. Illustrations and examples will be presented as to how these guides may be utilized effectively in mainstream college instruction in the curricula of the humanities and the natural and social sciences. This concluding perception of the coming of age in college instruction may be viewed as a response (in some wise) to the fervent plea from K. Patricia Cross (1976, *passim*, chapter one) for a revolution in college teaching.

Goals for the 1980s and 1990s:
The Coming of Age of College Instruction

In the final report of the Carnegie Council on Policy Studies in Higher Education (1980), a complex picture is presented of problems which will beset American higher education from the 1980s to the year 2000. The underlying generators of the future problems are: (1) an anticipated demographic depression of five to fifteen percent in college enrollment, (2) continuing escalating costs in financing college educational programs, and (3) an enlarged enrollment of nontraditional students. The report presents contrasting predictions for meeting the challenge of these problems which range from gloomy, pessimistic forecasts of threatened survival for some vulnerable institutions to relatively optimistic conjectures about resilient adaptations for successful continuance of other colleges. Permeating the entire report, however, is a clear, unequivocal summons for a redefinition of the role and mission of American higher education.

In the opinion of the Council, the colleges and universities which survive the next two decades in good shape are probably those which will recruit students most actively, admit students most readily, retain them most assiduously, counsel them most attentively, grade them most considerately, finance their students most adequately, teach them most conscientiously, and then place their graduates in jobs most insistently. In fact, the Council intimates that the American institutions of higher education which are most likely to endure successfully in the next twenty years are those that will take more and more the form and function of the community colleges in adjusting to the realities of the society.

To some extent, American higher education finds that it must plan for an unknown future. (And the risks involved in futurology do not have to be belabored.) Plato's ageless adage—"What is honored in a country will be cultivated there"—may have been a significant point of reference in the Carnegie Council report, for in it all institutions of higher education are urged to contemplate carefully their prospective futures and to determine the policies that will favorably affect them. *The importance of improving the quality of teaching in American higher education is given a rank of the highest priority in the Council's recommended courses of action in the next two decades.*

In the 1960s some factions in the student protest movement began to register their disenchantment with the academic policies and functions in American higher education; hindsight analyses reveal that the students were giving vent to their frustrations at American higher education becoming an educational commodities' market—a place in which knowledge and credentials are manufactured and retailed. (See Kerr, 1966, *passim*) Despite their inarticulate, frequently rowdy demonstrations, the 1960s student protesters were attempting to convey to their colleges and universities a message of extreme importance—that they wanted much more from the college experience than monodimensional information-processing; they wanted to develop the skills and competencies through which they could understand themselves and their world with increased meaning.

The general unreadiness in the 1960s of faculties across the nation to make a coherent, reasonable response to student dissent about academic affairs is now history. Superficial listening to student requests coupled with simplistic responses resulted generally in the abolition of many required courses in American colleges and universities. For many college faculties, the dissolution of degree requirements merely delayed temporarily the inexorable confrontation with problems of conducting meaningful teaching and learning with increasingly heterogeneous students.

On many campuses, as a result of student protest the courses which were frequently no longer required were the so-called "general education" courses. These courses had become since the 1930s the core of the first two-years in American undergraduate education and customarily consisted of interdisciplinary, broadly-based, survey or introductory studies of the major disciplines in higher educational studies—the humanities, and the natural and social sciences. These general education studies embodied the universals of human culture and the fundamental knowledge that any person who considered himself an educated person should possess in common with other educated persons. To paraphrase Whitehead (1968), the general education courses aimed to develop students' human capacity to attend experience;

sought to teach them to think against what is and to imagine otherness; guided them in proposing alternatives to being and in organizing experience, societies, economies, and politics.

Fortunately for American higher education, the pendulum in the late 1970s swung back to an acknowledgement of the worth of a unifying core of liberating intellectual experiences for all undergraduates prior to launching into their specialized programs of study. Led by Princeton and Harvard, higher educational institutions are revising and rededicating themselves to reinstituting general education as the cohesive instrument of undergraduate education. (Levine, 1979) And when taught with enthusiasm, imagination, and thoroughness, the general education studies provide the American college student the pluralistic development that he craves.

There is general agreement in higher educational circles that the humanities, the natural sciences, and the social sciences are essential elements of a liberal education, even though there is less agreement about the respective contributions of each area. It is the position in this monograph, however, that the humanities, the veritable mirror of human visions and perceptions of life, have an especially vital contribution to make to the pluralistic development of high-risk students as well as to all of today's undergraduates who reflect the "future shock" in this era of accelerating change. It is for this reason that in the next section of this monograph prototype instruction in the humanities will be presented as a highly desirable area of study for today's students who have particular need for nurturing. The guides for effective instruction in the humanities will illustrate ways in which mainstream curricula instruction can (and must) respond to the developmental needs of student populations today.

Prototype Instruction in the Humanities

Upon numerous occasions, Robert Maynard Hutchins is reported to have observed that the primary foci of the humanistic studies were to secure answers to the following questions: What is man? What is man's role and purpose in all of creation? What is man's destiny? Through the humanistic media—literature, philosophy, music, and the fine arts—individuals have communicated their visions, speculations, and interpretations of the human experience. And it is in this veritable storehouse of coded experiences that students may identify with, and respond to, and benefit from the full spectrum of the manifold aesthetic, imaginative, and ethical elements of human existence. (See Bush, 1966) Today, perhaps with a sense of urgency transcending any other period in its history, there is a critical need in American higher education for effective instruction in the humanities.

Literature, as the most direct and comprehensive expression of human concerns and the most generally accessible body of material, is selected for the purpose of this section. The guides for prototype instruction in literature that follow represent a synthesis of the principles of high-risk instruction presented in chapter four of this monograph (which are broadly applicable to mainstream instruction) with guides abstracted from exemplary college teaching activities as reported in *Effective Teaching* (Change, 1978).

1. *Effective instruction in literature in higher education rests initially upon a conscious recognition by teachers of the adulthood of most college students and of their voluntary (not captive) status as learners.* Freedom of choice in the learning interactions, therefore, must permeate all aspects of the instructional programs. Being continually mindful of the students' adult status while conducting learning activities in literature of necessity leads to teachers employing *multiple approaches while guiding students in understanding and interpreting literary works*. Teacher imposition of "the one best way" is *verboten*. Any of the interpretation strategies that follow are encouraged for use as a student's preferred technique; others are utilized upon occasion for the broadening of perspectives: impressionistic/personal analyses of a literary composition as well as historical/factual ones; analyses of the language and mode of a work as well as of the broader cultural context of it; criticism and evaluation of an author's personal/biographical identity as well as that of his socio-economic-political milieu; exhaustive analysis of a particular work of an author as well as globally analyzing (summatively) the totality of his contribution; and tracing the history of ideas—religious, philosophical, political, social, etc.—in a specified era through designated literary works as well as tracing the various ideas in one author's works during his entire productive years.

When students are provided opportunities for developing their preferred, analytical, literary skills, the sense of accomplishment gratifies their ego and generates increased intellectual and literary interest.

2. A corollary to the foregoing guide is the following: *Effective*

instruction in college literature today is predicated upon faculty understanding and acceptance of the vast experiential maturity and diversity of contemporary college students. Through television and other forms of the communications revolution, today's college student has been exposed to the full parameters of human experience. In a typical class of thirty students, in addition to the literary sources under study, there are ostensibly thirty other potential sources of impressions, beliefs, commitments, biases, perspectives, and the opinions on the vicissitudes or conditions which the *homo sapiens* encounters. *In prototype classes in literature, today, students are partners with the instructor and the text as sources of individual insight, knowledge, reflection, and intuition.* The sharing of one's personal vision and understanding of another's perception of a living episode is one of the truly satisfying educational interludes in college.

By greatly broadening the opportunities for student participation in class recitations and other sharing activities, student learning becomes increasingly a positive, active exercise over against the traditionally ineffectual, passive role.

3. Productive teaching and learning in college literature courses is found, also, under the aegis of teachers who comprehend and accept academic heterogeneity in their students. These teachers understand student differences in cognitive styles, learning proclivity, and especially in reading proficiency, and are able, therefore, to utilize a multiplicity of instructional strategies in order to cope fruitfully with student variability. *These effective literature teachers use diagnostic/prescriptive instruction in conjunction with multimedia and multimodel learning aids.*

Inasmuch as the study of literature is essentially the reading of literature with requisite comprehension, it is mandatory that the literature teacher have specific knowledge of student levels of reading proficiency. (In addition to the standard scores which the institution's admissions office or learning assistance program supplies, teachers today develop informal reading comprehension tests based on the textbooks which are actually being studied in the course. If the teacher does not possess the requisite competencies for devising such a screening measure, members of the institution's learning assistance center will have the necessary skill for performing this service. In Appendixes B, C, and D of this monograph are brief papers that supply relevant information regarding reading problems, issues, and instructional procedures in college.

After teachers have become informed about their students' general levels of reading proficiency, it is possible to "prescribe" appropriate supplementary texts, A-V materials, periodicals, self-pacing aids, etc. which are consonant with their diagnosed status in reading.

For example, do students need improvement in (1) comprehending figurative language, (2) identifying elements of the authors style, (3) understanding complex rhetorical structures, or (4) generalizing facts into a central idea? Identifying for students appropriate tutors as well as additional assistance for successful functioning in the literature course are services which are rendered today, also, by effective instructors in the mainstream college curricula. Frequently these services are given in consultation with the campus-wide learning assistance program.

A highly regarded instructional technique which is typical of successful literature teachers today (especially with academically heterogeneous students) involves the skillful use of an attribute called *cognitive flexibility*. By that term is meant an ability to expatiate and illustrate a complex, archaic, or abstruse concept with seemingly endless, meaningful, redundant allusions and examples. Coupled with this skill in what may be called *synonymity*, effective literature teachers have mastered, also, the use of the metaphor and analogy. (Bountiful, explicit, direct comparisons between unfamiliar things and familiar ones pay great dividends in student comprehension.) And in this era in which many students do limited amounts of sustained, wide reading, extending their vocabularies through concomitant learning by this operative technique is a highly desirable instructional bonus. (See Appendix F for the Directed Reading Activity [DRA] Adapted to College Studies.)

4. Effective instruction in literature herein recommended for the 1980s and 1990s includes student attainment of objectives and goals other than those in the cognitive domain. These nonsubject matter goals and objectives increasingly are being accepted in responsive circles and have merit equal to that of monodimensional content-mastery. The development of interpersonal skills as well as skills in handling realia feasibly and creatively are necessary for balanced

living in the kind of world in which we now find ourselves. And the field of literature is especially well-suited to serve as a medium in college through which holistic, pluralistic development may transpire. *Productive literature courses in today's higher education include a constellation of learning activities which satisfy pluralistic objectives and goals—some cognitive, some interpersonal, and others that involve realia (material things).*

With the publication of *The School and the Society* in 1900, John Dewey became the single, greatest continuing influence in American elementary and secondary education. His beliefs that the ideal school reflects the character of the larger society and that education at its best is life itself, transformed the very foundations of American education. Of equal importance to the foregoing views was Dewey's belief that education is most productive when it is an active endeavor; and that, in effect, *learning is doing*. Thus for some seven decades, elementary and seondary education in America has regularly utilized various and sundry learning strategies in which students were involved in "acting-out," participatory, "doing" activities.

Within the past fifteen years of increased awareness in American higher education of the need for effective instruction to meet student diversity, slowly but surely evidence may be found in colleges and universities of a gradual infiltration of Dewey's "learning-by-doing" philosophy. Today in some of the most respected citadels in higher education, there are courses (especially in the humanities and social sciences) in which *"games": simulations, role-playing, mimicry, contests, student projects,* and *graphic models and miniatures* are developed to concretize and reinforce the course content. (See ERIC on TE, 1979; and Miller, 1979 *passim.*)

Employing multidimensional learning strategies in literature, for example, provides students with a variety of avenues through which to attain the legitimate goals of the course. Those students who are particularly adept at verbal information-processing may need very little other than the textbook and related references in order to conceptualize a literary work or epoch. On the other hand, there are students for whom the verbal text does not come alive fully until some audiovisual-motor involvement figuratively breathes life into the text. For both types of students, there are intellectual and interpersonal dividends to be derived from collaboratively developing a dramatic, literary episode to share with their classmates.

Games and *play* have manifold historical connotations in all great civilizations, and the fact that their potential is now being recognized in higher educational instruction is a welcomed innovation. Associated with an acceptance of "gaming" in college instruction is a commitment in some wise to the efficacy of holistic student development. In essence, college instructors are coming of age and are evidencing concern for and committing themselves to other than monodimensional learning.

A Final Word

It is customary in the waning days of a year for national weekly news magazines as well as the distinguished daily, metropolitan newspapers to publish end-of-the-year retrospective articles accompanied by look-ahead predictions. As 1979 rapidly approached its termination, perhaps because it was the turn of a decade, *Newsweek* (19 November, 1979) among other popular American print media, devoted an entire issue to taking stock of the 1970s. The thesis statement in the *Newsweek* issue was that the 1970s were ten years that shook the *Weltanschauung* and *Zeitgeist* of the national life in America more fundamentally than any previous decade in its history. (One has only to recall a few of the typical, unexpected, and overwhelming events: the war in Indochina, the oil embargo, the women's liberation movement, Skylab I, the Attica Penitentiary riot, the Watergate scandal, the resignation of President Nixon, the jogging and self-improvement fads, streaking, the People's Temple mass suicide in Guyana, and the Iran hostage dilemma.)

Whether through happenstance or design, the final report by the Carnegie Council on Policy Studies in Higher Education (1980) was presented early in 1980. In the report, not only is there an analytical assessment of American higher education in the 1970s, but there is, also, anticipatory historical forecasting about possible issues and problems facing colleges and universities in the next two decades and recommendations for coping with them. Inasmuch as higher education is not an isolated entity but is instead inextricably involved in and reflective of the larger society, the dislocations and stresses of the culture as a whole of necessity become part and parcel of higher education's issues and problems.

In spite of the fact that futurology is a booming enterprise in the Western world today, and that think-tanks have sprung up in every region of America manned with their own corps of "experts" who assist the government as well as industry in making critical decisions, predicting the future with any degree of accuracy remains a risky business.

It is probably for the preceding reason that the Carnegie Council presented both an optimistic scenario and a pessimistic one of American higher education from now to the year 2000. The astronomical number of variables that may affect higher education simply make firm prognostication visionary; nonetheless, a combination of knowledge, clearly defined goals, and rational imagination can offset mindless predictions and prevent pessimistic forecasts from becoming true.

The Carnegie Council report makes a central plea to American higher education which is reflected throughout this monograph. It is an uncompromising call for a redefinition of the role and mission of higher education in America. The concatenation of events in the *fin de siècle* of the twentieth century are proving to be as disorienting and cataclysmic as was the comparable epoch at the end of the nineteenth century. And even as the larger society is having to assume new approaches and techniques for coping with change, so must higher education adjust and adapt to the new demands. In both domains there is an urgent need for innovative, creative, dynamic retooling for new tasks and services as well as creative revisions in the use of old and present resources.

This monograph as well as the Carnegie Council report stresses the critical need for the development and sensitive utilization of instructional systems that can effectively meet the learning styles of academically diverse students. In each report the improvement of teaching deservedly was given priority of the highest order in the 1980s and 1990s. But there is another educational concern that was addressed neither in the Carnegie report nor in this monograph, yet to which some attention must be given. It is highly relevant to any discussion of the future improvement of American higher education. It concerns the role that higher education must and should assume in assisting elementary and secondary education in upgrading their learning programs.

The serious magnitude of academic underpreparation for higher education in America must (and can) stop. The type of postindustrial culture in which we now find ourselves requires a citizen who possesses a repertory of intellectual, social and personal competencies which have to be mastered at appropriate levels in the various developmental stages. Each level of public education, therefore, must make its own unique contribution in the overall educative process. Attempting as we now do to "educate from the top down" instead of from "the bottom up" is both wasteful and nonsensical. Surely it is time to tap the vast intellectual storehouses in American higher education to engage in imaginative efforts to ameliorate this nadir in elementary and secondary education.

In the *Third Wave*, Alvin Toffler (1980), the noted futurist, argues that in today's world the industrial system is collapsing under the impact of historic change. The crises of our times are affecting all major societal organizations and systems, and in effect there is a "third wave" civilization breaking upon us. This new civilization will generate a new and more humanly rewarding type of life. (Toffler characterizes the "first wave" civilization as having come into being about 100,000 years ago, when man developed the system of agriculture; and the "second wave" civilization as coming into being about 300 years ago, with the emergence of the Industrial Revolution.)

Toffler believes that the coming of the "third wave" will generate the development of a "new man." An important factor in the development of the "new man" will be the institution of a new conceptualization of the acculturation and educative processes. Central to the new philosophy of education will be a serious break with compulsory, authoritarian, hierarchical, bureaucratic, mass educational practices. The "new education" and "acculturation" will produce a citizen with a heightened sense of his humanity and individuality who is more interested in developing his special perceptions and talents than in deferring gratification solely for economic self-sufficiency.

The departure from the present educational commitment in America which has been based upon the Protestant work ethic, Toffler foretells, will bring about a similar demise of the linear view of the "good life." The educational system that will replace the status quo will be inextricably interwoven and interspersed with work and life, and will transpire in many settings and throughout life in places other than the traditional schoolhouse. The linear view of education and life will then be superseded by a *Gestalten* (configuration) mode in which multiple, simultaneous, and parallel experiences will be lived. The ultimate aim of education for the "new man" is to produce an individual who has a sense of "balance"—one who is comfortable with the abstract as well as with the concrete; with handiwork as well as with headwork; with work as well as with play; with objectivity as well as with subjectivity; one who can balance his productive enterprises with his consumption activities; and one who can balance other-directedness with inner-directedness.

In some ways this entire monograph has been a statement about the necessity for American higher education to get about the business of developing instructional systems that will contribute to the development of "new learners" for the "third wave" civilization. The case for improved college teaching as presented in this instructional paradigm for high-risk college students, tersely summarized, is this: In meeting the challenge today for effective college education while caught between the "second" and "third wave" civilizations, American higher education, through utilizing instructional systems committed to the pluralistic (holistic) philosophy presented herein, should be able to develop students who acquire "balanced" coping repertoires.

Appendix A

SYLLABUS IN BASIC ENGLISH/THRESHOLD LEVEL

Introduction

The verbal course in the Center for Academic Reinforcement (CAR) is designed for the first-time-in-college student (FTICS) who has unrealized potential in basic English writing skills. It is intended to bring about a positive attitude in the student's approach to writing and to help him acquire flexible mastery of those basic verbal skills which are essential in his current scholastic endeavors and in his later career activities.

Through planned systematic instruction, the verbal course helps the student to develop and share his ideas effectively and intelligibly in a logically organized written form. The global focus of the course is the development of unified, coherent paragraphs that can be embedded successfully in written compositions. Two levels of instruction run concurrently through the semester. Level A encompasses the writing of well-constructed sentences; and Level B develops the organizing of unified, coherent paragraphs.

While the approach to Level A is primarily didactic, the approach to Level B is largely heuristic. The student is encouraged to listen for ideas, read for ideas and share his ideas orally. He then discovers that the graphic symbol of writing is simply a fusion of his aural, visual, and oral skills.

Although the paragraph is used in various types of discourse—argumentation, narration, description, and exposition—the verbal course emphasizes the development of the type of paragraph to be used in exposition. The expository paragraph, therefore, is given in-depth development, for it is the basic unit of essays and textbooks written in science, engineering, philosophy, and other academic fields. Because the expository paragraph is the tool the student will use to relate facts, explain theories, define terms, compare ideas and associate causes and effects, its development is the nucleus of the Verbal course.

*This material is abridged and adapted from "Syllabus of the Verbal Component," 1979 (The Center for Academic Reinforcement, Howard University, Washington, D.C. 20059).

CAR-V: General Performance Objectives*

At the conclusion of the CAR-V course, the student will be able to:

1. discuss the interrelatedness of the communication skills as a basis for improving writing;
2. use phonemic and morphemic analysis as an aid to understanding vocabulary development;
3. classify words according to their forms and functions and determine their uses in sentences;
4. demonstrate how the basic sentences are formed, how modifying words and phrases are added to those sentences, and how clauses are combined to form sentences that communicate ideas;
5. demonstrate the use of correct punctuation, mechanics, and spelling in writing;
6. correct the most common structural faults in sentence writing: faulty agreement of subject-verb and of pronoun-antecedent, faulty case and reference of pronouns, dangling and misplaced modifiers, faulty parallelism, shifts in point of view;
7. display a consciousness of effective diction in writing and speaking by distinguishing formal and informal levels of usage.
8. identify the common forms of expository paragraphs: analogy, analysis, cause and effect, comparison or contrast, definition, example, factual detail;
9. develop unified and coherent expository paragraphs; create effective topic sentences and supporting details, use transitions and connectives effectively;

10. make critical assessments of his own paragraphs as well as those of his classmates.

CAR-V: Specific Performance Objectives (Level A, 1-7; Level B, 8-15)

At the termination of Level A the student will be able to:

1. demonstrate a knowledge of the forms and functions of words;
2. demonstrate an understanding of the functional elements of a sentence;
3. construct various sentence patterns and expand them through the correct use of phrases and clauses;
4. use the processes of coordination and subordination to join and embed sentences;
5. determine and illustrate the correct use of punctuation marks in grammatical constructions;
6. identify and construct sentences with related ideas arranged logically and coherently;
7. decode unfamiliar words by an analysis of their roots, prefixes, and suffixes.

At the termination of Level B the student will be able to:

8. substitute overworked words with synonyms drawn from his repertoire of related words;
9. identify different forms of discourse;
10. arrange ideas according to their levels of generality from the general terms to the more specific terms;
11. develop topic sentences which will provide unity and focus for the paragraph;
12. organize supporting details by giving an order or a combination of order to the ideas;
13. use a variety of methods to develop expository paragraphs;
14. evaluate expository paragraphs for unity, support, and coherence;
15. develop various paragraphs to be used in the essay: introductory, body, transitional, and concluding and synthesize them into a finished essay.

CAR-V Instructional Units

LEVEL A: WRITING WELL-CONSTRUCTED SENTENCES

Unit One: Forms and Functions of Words
—Number, case, tense
—Parts of speech
Unit Two: Parts of the Sentence
—Basic sentence patterns
—modifying elements
—Phrases
—Clauses
Unit Three: Coordination and Subordination of Sentences
Unit Four: Punctuation of Sentences
—Internally
—Terminally
Unit Five: Sentence Conventions
—Agreement of subject and verb
—Agreement of reference of pronoun
—Point of view
Unit Six: Common Sentence Errors
—Fragments
—Shifts in point of view
—Faulty parallelism
—Dangling and misplaced elements
—Run-on/fused sentence
—Comma splice
Unit Seven: Four approaches to vocabulary development
—Through related words
—Through words derived from Latin and Greek roots
—Through words borrowed from other languages
—Through the forming of derivatives

Unit Seven applies to both Levels A and B and is ongoing through the semester. Because of time constraint, the approaches to vocabulary development will be discussed, assignments will be made for independent study, and a mastery quiz will be administered every week.

LEVEL B: ORGANIZING UNIFIED, COHERENT PARAGRAPHS

Unit One: Writing—the fusing of ideas from listening, reading, and verbalizing
Unit Two: Introducing different kinds of discourse with emphasis on exposition
Unit Three: Constructing topic sentences that give direction and limit the writer—controlling idea
Unit Four: Identifying levels of generality in general and in specific terms
Unit Five: Developing paragraphs through the ordering of the supporting sentences
Unit Six: Using different methods of development to write expository paragraphs
Unit Seven: Achieving unity and support in paragraphs
Unit Eight: Achieving coherence in paragraphs
Unit Nine: Developing the different kinds of paragraphs used in essays and theses

CAR-V: Instructional Strategies

PROCEDURES

1. A diagnostic composition test is administered to determine the overall writing proficiency of each student. The results of this test in conjunction with information from required admissions tests (SAT-V and Test of Standard Written English, CEEB) decide the general placement in the CAR-V program.

2. CAR-V "in-house" tests that are more specifically diagnostic are also administered to determine whether the student should begin with sentence writing or with paragraphs. The in-house tests identify specific deficiencies in the mechanics of English.

3. Individual "prescriptions" are developed for each student based upon his test batteries, and his directed instruction as well as his independent and quasi-independent laboratory-learning programs are outlined.

4. Unit and modular tests determine student progress and ultimate termination in the course.

Schema of CAR-V Course

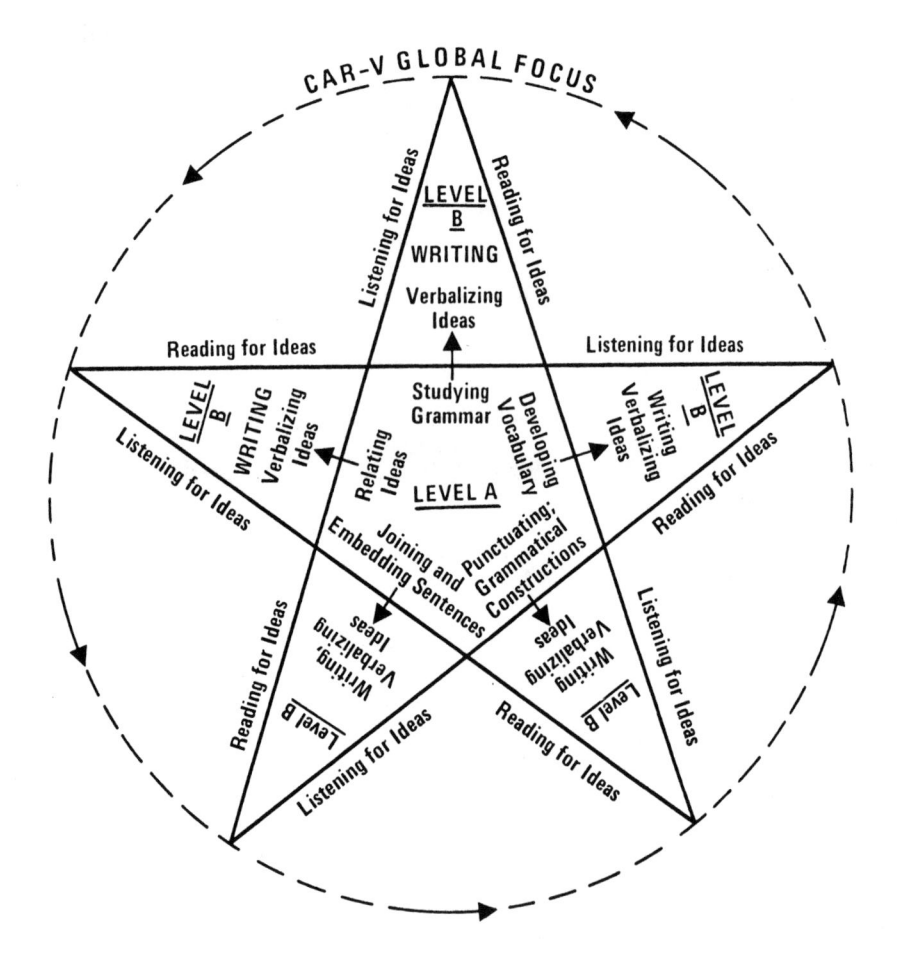

5. There is a synergetic relationship between diagnosed student needs, prescribed areas of study, the materials of instruction, the techniques of instruction, and the evaluation of student progress.

LEARNING ACTIVITIES

The learning activities are an amalgam of didactic, heuristic, self-paced, independent, quasi-independent, multimedia, multimodal, compressed-time learning interactions. Any of the following instructional practices are utilized: lectures, class discussions, programmed learning, computer, peer-tutoring, independent laboratory study with audiovisual, nonprint, and mechanical devices, and collaborative team-study.

Appendix B

THE LITERATE DEMANDS OF A TYPICAL COLLEGE TEXTBOOK

The typical college textbook poses prodigious problems for the freshman who enters higher education with insufficient development in the verbal tools of learning. The first-time-in-college student needs to possess (1) an adequate vocabulary, (2) a repertory of vocabulary acquisition skills, (3) a variety of rates-of-reading, as well as (4) flexible, mature reading comprehension strategies for college-level study. Without these proficiencies, he will be overwhelmed by the precise, abstruse diction, the complex syntactical structures, and the hierarchical organization of the majority of college textbooks.

College instructors of high-risk students may become sensitized to their students' reading problems through reviewing the verbal challenges of a representative textbook. *Psychology and Life* (Floyd L. Ruch and Philip G. Zimbardo, 9th ed. Glenview, Il.: Scott, Foresman and Company, 1975) is a widely adopted college text used customarily in the first (introductory or survey) course in psychology in colleges throughout the United States. Its organizational and expository features typify the present genre in American college textbook writing, and optimum success in studying it requires that the student possess a veritable constellation of reading/thinking/study skills.

An analysis of *Psychology and Life* follows, and it should alert the unwary college instructor to the literate demands of a typical college textbook.

Chapters (16). The number of chapters has been attuned to the conventional sixteen-week semester for a chapter-per-week assignment. The chapters range from twenty-six to forty-six pages and average thirty-thousand-words-plus (30,000+). At a study-reading rate of 300 words-per-minute, the student must spend 104 to 184 minutes (1 3/4 hours to 3 hours plus) to read one chapter. The taking of notes, underlining, abstracting, and other study-reinforcement activities will necessarily lengthen the reading time.

Pages (788 double-columned). There are approximately 600,000-plus running words in the main body of the text followed by twenty-one pages of a glossary of 800 specialized terms. Each page contains 800 to 1,000 words (depending upon the size and number of graphic illustrations). A twenty-eight page appendix on "Basic Concepts in Statistics" and references round out the text. The overall size is that of a standard, college-size dictionary.

Syntactical Structures. The majority of the sentences are twenty-five to thirty-five words in length—about twice as long as the sentence in current American periodical and news publications. The sentences abound in complex structures—adjectives and adverbial phrases and clauses in appositive relationships; inverted elements; compound-complex and complex sentences, etc. The foregoing syntax requires that the student has flexible control of standard English.

Paragraph Development. There are 205 paragraphs in the average chapter. Based upon an estimation of three to five supporting details in each paragraph, each chapter contains approximately 600 to 1,000 significant ideas in support of one of the 205 principal concepts. Thus, in the main body of the text alone, there are approximately 3,500 to 4,000 key concepts supported by 15,000 to 20,000 explanatory details. In spite of the fact that the paragraphs are developed in an exemplary manner, the obvious burden of "fact-saturation" demands that the student possess a productive fund of reading/thinking/study skills for fact mastery and retrieval.

Graphic and Typographical Aids. A multiplicity of charts, graphs, pictures, and typographies of great diversity abound throughout the text to illustrate and concretize the nomenclature and abstruse concepts and terms. The various typographies—bold-face type, italics, colored type, etc.—give the reader ample cues and clues to meaning. The charts and graphs—bar, line, picture, histo—in black and white as well as in color, often require sophisticated mathematical and graphic interpretation skills for successful understanding.

Readability. By utilizing Edward Fry's "Graph for Estimating Readability Extended" (to the seventeenth level—graduate school writings), it was possible to calculate the grade-level of difficulty of

Psychology and Life. Based upon the criteria of "average sentence length" and "average number of syllables per 100 words," the text is approximately *fourteenth grade readability level*.

Despite Fry's contention that high motivation overcomes high readability level and that low motivation demands a low readability level, even the motivated college freshman who possesses immature literate skills will find the *Psychology and Life* text a challenge. (See Edward Fry, "Fry's Readability Graph: Clarifications, Validity, and Extension to Level 17." *Journal of Reading*, Vol. 21, #3 (Dec., 1977, pp. 242-252).

The foregoing brief review of some of the essential features of a widely adopted, standard college textbook may sensitize instructors to the verbal coping skills such a book demands. Multiply, if you will, the demands of *Psychology and Life* by three to five other texts of comparable difficulty in different disciplines which the student will be using during a typical semester. The staggering reading assignments may easily reach 150,000 words per week.

Under the sheer weight of these literate requirements, it is reported that even the highly motivated student who happens to be fully prepared for higher education is sorely pressed to make the first years in college productive—both personally and intellectually. For the student who is underprepared for college—especially one who has impeding underdevelopment in verbal skills—the reading demands of the initial semesters may be virtually insuperable. The need is clear, therefore, for college instructors who not only understand the student's problem, but are prepared and willing to provide the requisite academic support.

Appendix C

LEVELS AND DIMENSIONS OF READING COMPREHENSION APPLICABLE TO ALL TYPES OF DISCOURSE

Whether or not the reader is engaged in securing meaning from written discourse in the humanities, the natural sciences, or the social sciences, he is called upon to activate a veritable constellation of verbal thought-getting processes. Teachers on all levels of education should have an understanding of the aggregate, variegated, verbal/thinking skills which comprise efficient comprehension, and should be able to guide their students in the development of a full spectrum of them.

The statements that follow synthesize and summarize widely recognized views on the levels and dimensions of reading comprehension:

1. Comprehending what is read is not a unitary, general act or ability; rather, it embraces a multiplicity of different skills.
2. Some of the principal thought-getting skills required in reading comprehension and interpretation are:
    a. Getting the main idea and supporting details (literal comprehension) in phrases, sentences, and different types of paragraphs
    b. Getting implied ideas (inferential comprehension) in phrases, sentences, and different types of paragraphs
    c. Comprehending the multiple meanings of words (denotations, connotations) in phrases, sentences, and different types of paragraphs

- d. Comprehending diverse structures and functions of words: content words (nouns, verbs, adjectives, etc.) *versus* tool words (prepositions, articles, conjunctions, etc.)
- e. Recognizing and discriminating between judgments, inferences, and facts
- f. Interpreting figurative language: simile, metaphor, litotes, hyperbole, etc.
- g. Interpreting idiomatic language: slang, cant, colloquialisms, etc.
- h. Forming and reacting to sensory images
- i. Anticipating outcomes
- j. Developing the basic techniques of critical reading
- k. Generalizing, summarizing, and organizing ideas
   - (1) Making logical judgments and drawing conclusions
   - (2) Comparing and contrasting ideas
   - (3) Perceiving relationships: of time, space, sequence, cause-effect, class, whole-part, analogous, general-specific, abstract-concrete
   - (4) Identifying the author's point of view
   - (5) Identifying elements of style: 1st person, 3rd person, flash-back, etc.
   - (6) Understanding the basic rhetorical techniques: anecdotes, quotations, illustrations, argumentation, etc.
- l. Understanding foreign words, phrases, and abbreviations frequently used in English exposition
- m. Recognizing literary devices: satire, irony, cynicism, etc.
- n. Using graphic aids in understanding exposition: maps, graphs, charts, etc.
- o. Comprehending the structural-thematic organization of: a chapter, an article, a textbook

3. To some extent, the mental processes involved in reading comprehension have a prepotent relationship—i.e., some skills must be mastered before others may be understood and used effectively (e.g., being able to get the literal meaning of a passage or the main idea must be mastered before one can evaluate the effectiveness of the author's purpose or intent).

Conclusions

1. Guided practice in paragraph comprehension in all disciplines under the instructor's direct supervision is a highly recommended way to improve comprehension development. (Students should be encouraged to develop simple diagrams of the structure of a paragraph.) The main thought ("key" thought) could be represented horizontally, and its supporting details could be listed perpendicularly to the main thought. For the students who are especially deficient in the cues and clues to understanding rigid exposition, the instructor may have to begin with locating the "key" noun (or nominal) in the independent clause of the main sentence.

2. The instructor who develops provocative and evocative questions which motivate students to think in terms of *why* and *for what* as well as in terms of *who, when, where,* and *what* will guide the development of reading comprehension effectively. Similarly, the instructor who asks the students to *trace, describe, illustrate, compare,* and/or *contrast* will be conducting more significant reading/thinking processes than one who customarily asks students only to "tell what you read about."

3. Students should be encouraged and taught to use a study/reading formula such as SQ3R or PQ4R. Through regularly employing the survey and preview steps in the formula, students establish a useful framework-of-reference for understanding the passage prior to the actual reading of it. This framework gives the reader a dimension of familiarity with the subject which aids in comprehension.

Appendix D

THE DIRECTED READING ACTIVITY (DRA) ADAPTED TO COLLEGE STUDIES

For the better part of this century, elementary school methodologies have included guides for the classroom teacher to be used directly in assisting pupils in textbook reading. Popularly known as "the directed reading activity" (DRA), this multifaceted method has become firmly established on the elementary level as the principal instructional strategy in developing textbook reading proficiency.

Beginning in the late 1940s, when the "reading problem" became omnipresent in American secondary schools, and continuing until today when institutions of higher education are beset similarly with the problem, the need was and is evident for postelementary school developmental reading methods. It is the position in this paper that the DRA is especially adaptable to secondary and postsecondary school populations who need systematic assistance in reading successfully highly structured textbooks.

Over the years, the DRA's dominant features have become virtually standardized and constitute an amalgam of didactic and heuristic developmental reading techniques. It is believed that inherent in this blend of developmental reading processes lies its broad applicability to immature and mature learners alike, as well as to simple or complex rhetoric. The conventional instructional steps in the DRA are:

1. *Developing Readiness*—orientation for reading the selection. (a) establishing contact with the student's past knowledge of the topic; (b) clarifying "new" words and concepts; (c) stimuating interest

in reading the selection; (d) setting purposes for reading; (e) speculating about the possible nature of the selection; and (f) classifying and categorizing the type of material.

2. *Guided Reading*—directed silent reading to secure specific answers to pivotal questions. (a) posing questions related to the main theme or idea prior to those relating to the supporting details; (b) asking questions which demand factual, inferential, experiential, and vocabulary interpretations; (c) monitoring difficulties encountered by the students relating to vocabulary identification and/or conceptual understanding; and (d) encouraging diversity, yet validity, in interpreting the text.

3. *Directed Comprehension and Vocabulary Development*—(a) employing a variety of vocabulary development activities to reinforce the recognition and mastery of troublesome words identified in Step 2 above (picture, configuration, and context clues; phonetic and structural analysis; dictionary referral); (b) extending explanations and interpretations of difficult incidents or information in the text; (c) directing critical assessment of the text in light of pre-established purposes for reading; and (d) establishing purposes for re-reading or reinforcing activities.

4. *Rereading/Reviewing/Reinforcing*—strengthening understandings and increasing the mechanics of oral and silent reading. (a) providing opportunities for developing versatility and flexibility in interpretation; (b) guiding the re-reading and reviewing to increase enjoyment, find specific information, resolve an interpretation problem, to entertain others, and/or to savor the material; and (c) focusing upon possible areas of the material which may be explored further in independent study.

5. *Elaborative and Follow-up Activities*—spin-offs and fall-out from the textbook reading which lead to independent reading/study activities on related subjects. (a) relating the text material to supplementary readings; (b) utilizing dramatization, excursions, graphic representations, and written compositions as media for extending comprehension and mastery of the text readings; (c) taking notes and summarizing the principal concepts for future use; and (d) performing various workbook exercises, assignments, and research activities which reinforce the new concepts, information, and/or vocabulary of the textbook.

For the past seven years in a graduate course in reading methods, "Teaching Adults Read" (The School of Education, Howard University), the writer guided enrollees in modifying the elementary school DRA for use with secondary, postsecondary, and adult/continuing student populations. Over this period of time, various revisions in the five-step DRA were made and finally decided upon in an effort to attain a compact postelementary, developmental paradigm for textbook reading. Enrollees in the course field-tested the effectiveness of the adapted DRA through critiquing in-class simulations as well as in on-the-job reading lessons.

The revisions made in the five-step DRA resulted in a three-step version that encompasses significant principles of andragogy embodying effective techniques for guiding adult learning. The three-step DRA for mature learners (TS/DRA/ML) advocates unfailing teacher recourse to the student's, experiential background in the development of vocabulary, reading/study skills, and content comprehension. It encourages divergency in cognitive styles, and additionally, it focuses upon assisting the student regularly in seeking the relationships and possible applicability of textbook abstractions to immediate academic concerns and long range career goals.

In a word, the compact DRA attempts to blend the essence of "confluent education" with productive textbook reading strategies for the mature learner—an integration that fuses the cognitive, affective, readiness/awareness, and motivational domains into one meaningful gestalt.

The remedial/developmental (R/D) teacher in today's intitutions of higher education must cope frequently with the new entrant who lacks requisite skills for independent college reading. Especially in the initial semesters of study, the underprepared freshman requires targeted guidance to meet the demands of standard college textbooks. In the humanities as well as in the natural or social sciences, the R/D college instructor may find the following TS/DRA/ML to be an effective developmental aid:

1. *Structured preview*—bridging the gap between the known and the unknown; orientating and goal setting; arousing and capturing interest; challenging and motivating.

This step is an open-ended colloquy between instructor and students; in essence, it is a "prologue" in which a focused, preliminary introduction to the text-to-be-read is discussed. Students are encouraged to recall latent and residual knowledge and understand the new material as "pump-priming" for it. Exceptional elements of organization and exposition are noted; abstruse vocabulary, nomenclature, and concepts are clarified; and the instructor guides the students in establishing specific purposes for reading/studying the selection. (*N.B.* This step may be conducted entirely in a face-to-face oral interchange between instructor and students, or it may involve a guided review of a teacher-prepared, written "study guide." Hopefully, before the end of the semester, the students should be able to develop their own "structured preview" for assigned readings.)

2. *Directed overview*—targeting thesis ideas through pivotal questioning; preempting potential comprehension problems through a systematic survey technique.

In Step 2, the students' comprehension and interpretation of the text are assisted through purposive, provocative, challenging questions which lead them to seek answers to significant ideas. The students' regular employment of a study/reading formula, such as SQ3R or PQ4R, forestalls the development of vocabulary and comprehension difficulties and encourages flexibility in reading rates. A repertory of vocabulary building and comprehension skills are applied by the students as the nature of the text demands.

It is important in this step that the instructor cultivate the students' skill in moving consistently from literal interpretations to inferential, and then to creative (applicational) thinking about whatever is read.

3. *Independent reinforcement and extension*—recapitulating, recasting, editing; reclassifying and recategorizing; organizing and integrating; individualizing and personalizing.

In this concluding step, the students utilize a variety of organizational study/reading/writing processes, amenable to their cognitive styles, to insure appropriate immediate and delayed use of important concepts in the text. Different types of note-taking, underlining, and summarizing are employed to insure effective, meaningful information storage and retrieval.

Supplementary readings and related references are consulted also, as specialized student interests emerge. Non-print media are resorted to regularly to amplify and/or concretize abstractions.

Conclusion

As R/D programs increasingly become integral parts of traditional institutions of higher education, the need is evident for these programs of study to have feasible, rational, productive methodologies for their clients. The TS/DRA/ML herein presented is highly malleable, and may be molded to accommodate both student academic heterogeneity and subject matter diversity.

In whatever future adaptations will be made in the TS/DRA/ML, the R/D instructor should remember that the ultimate goal of this study-reading guide is that the student will incorporate its basic procedures as a regular part of his repertory of indepedent learning skills.

References

Allen, Henry, "The Big 70's Burnout," *The Washington Post*, December 6, 1979, C1 and C15.

Ball, S., "Research and Program Evaluation: Some Principles, Precepts, and Practices," in the *Final Report of National Project II, Alternatives to the Revolving Door*. New York: Bronx Community College, n.d.

Ball, S., and S. B. Anderson. *Practices in Program Evaluation: A Survey and Some Case Studies*. Princeton, N. J.: Educational Testing Service, 1975.

Blake, Elias et al. *Degrees Granted and Enrollment Trends in Historically Black Colleges*. Washington, D. C.: Institute for Services to Education, 1974.

Breen, P., T. Donlon, and U. Whitaker, "The Learning and Assessment of Interpersonal Skills: Guidelines for Administrators and Faculty," *CAEL Working paper #4*. Princeton, N. J.: ETS, 1975.

Briggs, Leslie J. ed. *Instructional Design: Principles and Applications*. Englewood Cliffs, N. J.: Educational Technology Publications, 1979.

Brubacher, J. S., and W. Rudy. *Higher Education in Transition: A History of American Colleges and Universities 1636-1976*. 3rd. ed. New York: Harper and Row, 1976.

Bush, Douglas, "The Humanities." *The Contemporry University: USA*, Boston: Beacon Press, 1966, 186-205.

Butler, John H., and Theresa J. Jacoby. *Higher Grades Through Better Notes*. Belmont, CA: Fearson Published, 1965.

Canby, Henry S. *Alma Mater*. New York: Farrar, Straus, and Giroux, 1936.

Carkhuff, R. R. *Helping and Human Relations: A Primer for Lay and Professional Helpers*. 2 vols. New York: Holt, 1969.

Carman, R. A., "Cost-Effectiveness Analysis of Various Methods of Instruction in Developmental Mathematics," *Santa Barbara, California: Seminar Paper*, 1971.

Carnegie Council on Policy Studies in Higher Education. *Three Thousand Futures: The Next 20 Years for Higher-Education*. San Francisco: Jossey-Bass, Inc., 1980. Center for Research on Learning and Teaching. Memorandum to the Faculty, No. 48 (April 1972); No. 50 (December 1972);

No. 52 (October 1973); No. 55 (May 1975); No. 61 (December 1978). Ann Arbor: The University of Michigan.

Change Magazine. "Report on Teaching" (Report #1, March 1976; Report #2, July 1976; Report #3, January 1977; Report #4, July 1977; Report #5, January 1978). New Rochelle, N. Y.: Educational Change, Inc.

Change Magazine Press. *Guide to Effective Teaching*. New Rochelle, N.Y.: Change Magazine Press, 1978.

(The) *Chronicle* (of Higher Education). September 4, 1979, p. 17, Col. 2-4.

Clark, Kenneth B., "The Continuing Struggle to Desegregate U. S. Education," *The Chronicle of Higher Education*, September 4, 1979, p. 64.

Clowes, Darrel, "Form and Function," *Journal of Developmental and Remedial Education*, III, No. 1 (Fall 1979), 2-3, 13.

Cronbach, L. J., "How Can Instruction Be Adapted to Individual Differences?" in R. M. Gagne, ed., *Learning and Individual Differences*. Columbus, Ohio: Merrill, 1967.

Cross, K. Patricia. *Accent on Learning*. San Francisco: Jossey-Bass Publishers, 1976.

Cross K. Patricia. *Beyond the Open Door: New Students in Higher Education*. San Francisco: Jossey-Bass, 1971.

Cross, K. Patricia, "Education as a Super Highway," *Journal of Developmental and Remedial Education*, III, No. 2 (Winter 1979), 2-3, 32.

DeVane, William C., "The College of Liberal Arts," *The Contemporary University: U.S.A*. Boston: Beacon Press, 1964, 1-8.

ERIC Clearinghouse on Teacher Education. *Simulations and Games: An ERIC Bibliography*. Washington, D. C.: ERICTE, #1 Dupont Circle, 1979.

FIPSE. *The Proceedings of the Final Conference of National Project II: Alternatives to the Revolving Door*. Washington, D. C.: Fund for the Improvement of Postsecondary Education, 1976.

Friedman, Nathalie and James Thompson. *The Federal Educational Opportunity Grant Program: A Status Report Fiscal Year 1970*. Washington, D. C.: Educational Resources Information Center, 1971.

Gagne, R. M. and L. J. Briggs. *Principles of Instructional Design*. New York: Holt, Rinehart, and Winston, 1974.

Gardner, John. *Excellence: Can We Be Equal and Excellent Too?* New York: Harper, 1961.

Garms, Walter I., "A Benefit-cost Analysis of the Upward Bound Program," *Journal of Human Resources*, Vol. 8, 1975, 206-220.

Gesell, Arnold, H. M. Laverson, et al. *The First Five Years of Life*. New York: Harper and Row, 1940.

Gordon, Edmund W. *Opportunity Programs for the Disadvantaged in Higher Education*. Washington, D. C.: American Association for Higher Education, 1975.

Gould, Samuel B. *Diversity by Design*. Commission of Non-Traditional Study. San Francisco: Jossey-Bass, Inc., 1973, p. XV.

Grant, Katryn, and Daniel R. Hoeber. *Basic Skills Programs: Are They Work-

ing? AAHE-ERIC/Higher Education Research Report No. 1, 1978, Washington, D. C.: AAHE, 1978.

Hamilton, Edwin, "Black Colleges: Opportunity for Non-Traditional Study," *The Journal of Negro Education*, XLVI, No. 3 (Summer, 1977), 254-23.

Havighurst, R. *Human Development and Education*. New York: Longmans, Green, 1953.

Heimberer, Frederic, "The State Universities," *the Contemporary University: U.S.A.* Boston: Beacon Press, 1964.

Henderson, Vivian, "The Future of Black Colleges," *Journal of the Academy of Arts and Sciences*, C (Summer, 1971), 50-55.

Hill, J. E. *The Educational Sciences*. Bloomfield Hills, Michigan: Oakland Community College Press, 1971.

Horowitz, Irving L. and William Friedland. *The Knowledge Factory*. Chicago: Aldine, 1970.

Jencks, Christopher and David Riesman. *The Academic Revolution*. Garden City, N.Y.: Doubleday 1968.

Jones, H. E., "Intelligence and Problem Solving," *Handbook of Aging and the Individual*. Chicago: University of Chicago Press, 1959.

Karabel, J., "Community Colleges and Social Stratification," in *Educating the Disadvantaged*, Edited by E. laxman. New York: AMS Press, 1973.

Keller, F. S., "The Basic System," in F. S. Keller and J. G. Sherman, *The Keller Plan Handbook*. Menlo Park, CA: W. A. Benjamin, Inc., 1974.

Kerr, Clark., "The Frantic Race to Remain Contemporary," *The Contemporary University: U.S.A.* Boston: Beacon Press, 1964, 19-38.

Kerr, Clark. *The Uses of the University*. New York: Harper and Row, 1966.

Kidd, J. R., *How Adults Learn*. New York: Association Press, 1959, 1973.

Knowles, Malcom S. *The Adult Learner: Andragogy versus Pedagogy*. New York: The Macmillan Co., 1964.

Knox, Alan B. *Adult Development and Learning*. San Francisco: Jossey-Bass, 1977.

Kuhn, Thomas S. *The Structure of Scientific Revolutions*. Chicago: The University of Chicago Press, 1970.

Lee, Calvin B. T., ed. *Improving College Teaching*. Washington, D.C. American Council on Education, 1967.

Levine, Arthur. *Handbook on Undergraduate Curriculum: A Report for the Carnegie Council on Policy Studies in Higher Education*. San Francisco: Jossey-Bass, 1979.

Markle, S. M., "Programming and Programmed Instruction," In S. C. Tickton (ed.) *To Improve Learning: An Evaluation of Instructional Technology*. Vol. 1. New York: R. R. Bowker, 1970.

Maxwell, Martha. *Improving Student Learning Skills*. San Francisco: Jossey-Bass Publishers, 1979, *passim*.

Mayhew, Lewis B. *The Carnegie Commission on Higher Education*. San Francisco: Jossey-Bass, 1973, *passim*.

Mays, Benjamin. *Born to Rebel*. New York: Charles Scribner's Sons, 1971.

McClusky, Howard, "Central Hypotheses About Adult Learning," *Report of the Commission of the Professors of Adult Education*. Washington, D.C.: Adult Education Association of the U.S.A., 1958.

McGee, Leo and McAfee Dalton, "Role of the Traditionally Black Public Institumion of Higher Learning in Extension Education." *The Journal of Negro Education*, XLVI, No. 1 (Winter, 1977), pp. 46-52.

McLeish, J. *The Lecture Method*. Cambridge Monographs on Teaching Methods, No. 1. Cambridge, England: Cambridge Institute of Education, 1968.

McLuhan, Marshall. *The Gutenberg Galaxy*. Toronto: University of Tornoto Press, 1965.

Miller, David L. *Gods and Games*. New York: The World Publishing Company, 1979.

Miller, Harry L. *Teaching and Learning in Adult Education*. New York: The Macmillan Co., 1964.

Miller, LaMar P. and Edmund W. Gordon. *Equality of Educational Opportunity: A Handbook of Research*. New York: AMS Press, 1974.

Miltn, Ohmer. *Alternatives to the Traditional: How Professors Teach and How Students Learn*. San Francisco: Jossey-Bass, 1972.

Morison, Robert S., "Introduction," *The Contemporary University: USA*. Boston: Beacon Press, 1964.

Robert R. Moton Memorial Institute. *The Moton Guide to American Colleges With a Black Heritage*. Atlanta: Stein Printing Co., 1974, *passim*.

Mulka, M. J. and E. Sheevin. *An Evaluation of Policy Related Research on Post-Secondary Education for the Disadvantaged*. 2 vols. Washington, D.C.: National Science Foundaton, 1974.

Nelson, T. F., and D. W. Scott, "Personalized Instruction in Educational Psychology." In J. G. Sherman (ed.), *Personalized System of Instruction: 41 Germinal Papers*. Menlo Park, CA: W. A. Benjamin, Inc., 1974.

Newsweek. November 19, 1979.

Newton, Eunice Shaed, "Andragogy: Understanding the Adult as a Learner," *Journal of Reading*. XX, No. 5 (Fall 1977), 361-363.

O'Connell, Barry, "Where Does Harvard Lead Us?" *Change* (September 1978), 35-40, 61.

Olivas, Michael A. and Nan Alimba. *The Dilemma of Access—Minorities in Two-Year Colleges*. Washington, D.C.: Howard University Press, 1979.

Pauk, Walter. *How to Study in College*. Boston: Houghton Mifflin Co., 1974.

Prescott, Daniel. *The Child in the Educative Process*. New York: McGraw-Hill, 1957.

Proctor, Samuel D, "A Mind is a Terrible Thing to Waste," *Phi Delta Kappa*, November, 1978, 201s-203s.

Raywid, Mary Anne, "Models of the Teaching-Learning Situation," *Phi Delta Kappa* (April, 1977) 63-635.

Roszak, Theodore. *The Making of a Counter Culture*. Garden City, N. Y.: Doubleday, 1969.

Roueche, John E. and R. Wade Kirk. *Catching Up: Remedial Education*. San Francisco: Jossey-Bass, 1973.

Scandura, Joseph M. *Problem Solving: A Structural/Process Approach with Instructional Implications*. New York: Academic Press, 197.

Schwab, Joseph. *The College Curriculum and Student Protest*. Chicago: University of Chicago Press, 1969.

Sims, William E. "Guest Editorial: Black Colleges—Bicentennial Offers Little Hope," *The Journal of Negro Education*, XLV, No. 3 (Summer 1976). 21-224.

Suchman, Edward. *Evaluative Research: Principles and Practice in Public Service and Social Action Programs*. New York: Russell Sage Foundation, 1967.

Sullivan, L. L. *A Guide to Higher Education Learning Centers in the United States and Canada*. Portsmouth, N.H.: Entelek, 1978.

Thelen, Herbert A. *Dynamics of Groups at Work*. Chicago: University of Chicago Press, 1954.

Toffler, Alvin. *The Third Wave*. New York: William Morrow and Company, 1980.

Trent, J. W., and A. M. Cohen, "Research on Teaching in Higher Education," *Second Handbook of Research on Teaching*, R.M.W. Travers, ed. Chicago: Rand McNally, 1973.

United States Department of Labor. *Dictionary of Occupational Titles*. 2 vols. (3rd ed.). Washington, D.C.: U.S. Government Printing Office, 1965.

Van Doren, Mark. *Liberal Education*. Boston: Beacon Press, 1959.

Ward, Ben, "Learning Lab, Center Clinic? or What's in a Name?" *Journal of Developmental and Remedial Education*, Vol. 2, #3 (Spring 1979) 4-6.

Whitehead, Alfred North. *The Aims of Education and Other Essays*, New York: Free Press, 1968.

Willie, Charles V., and Cheater M. Hedgepeth. "The Educational Goals of Black Colleges." *Journal of Higher Education*, Vol. 50, No. 1, 1979, 90-95.

Wirtz, Willard, and others. *On Further Examinaion*. Report of the Advisory Panel on the Scholastic Aptitude Score Decline. Princeton, N.J.: College Entrance Examination Board, 1977.

Witkin, H. A., C. A. Moore, et. al. *Field-Dependent and Field-Independent Cognitive Styles and Their Educational Implications*. Princeton, N.J.: Educational Testing Service, 1975.

Witkin, H. A. *The Role of Cognitive Style in Academic Performance and in Teacher-Student Relations*. Princeton, N. J.: Educational Testing Service, 1973.